UNDERSTANDING

HOW TO ORDER:

Quantity discounts are available from the publisher, Prima Publishing & Communications, P.O. Box 1260UN, Rocklin, CA 95677; telephone **(916)786-0426**. On your letterhead include information concerning the intended use of the books and the number of books you wish to purchase.

U.S. Bookstores and Libraries: Please submit all orders to St. Martin's Press, 175 Fifth Avenue, New York, NY 10010; telephone (212) 674-5151.

UNDERSTANDING

Eliminating Stress and Finding Serenity in Life and Relationships

Jane Nelsen, Ed.D.

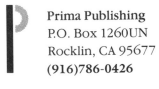

Prima Publishing
P.O. Box 1260UN
Rocklin, CA 95677
(916)786-0426

Typography by R. Nolan & Sons
Production by Bookman Productions
Cover design by The Dunlavey Studio

Prima Publishing & Communications
Rocklin, CA

Library of Congress Cataloging-in-Publication Data

Nelsen, Jane.
　　Understanding: eliminating stress and finding serenity in life and relationships.

　　Originally published: Fair Oaks, Calif.: Sunrise Press, © 1986.
　　1. Peace of mind.　2. Happiness.　3. Interpersonal relations.　4. Stress (Psychology)—Prevention.
I. Title.
BF637.P3N45　1988　　　158'.1　　　88-2547
ISBN 0-914629-72-7

88　89　90　91　RRD　10　9　8　7　6　5

Printed in the United States of America

This book is lovingly dedicated to my children
Terry
Jim
Ken
Brad
Lisa
Mark
and Mary
with the hope that they enjoy the buried treasure
within much sooner than I did.

Contents

1   A Treasure Map   5

2   Listening Softly   11

3   The Principle of Thinking as a Function   17
      Thinking from a Natural State of Mind or
         from a Programmed Thought System   20
      States of Thought   25

4   The Principle of Feelings as a Compass   27

5   The Principle of Separate Realities   33

6   The Principle of Mood Levels, or Levels of
    Consciousness   39
      Now You See It; Now You Don't   42
      Gratitude   43

7   What Now?   47
      Quiet   52
      So What? Big Deal! Who Says?   53
      Suggestions   54

8   What Thoughts Are You Willing to Give Up
    Your Happiness For?   57

Which Principle Is the Most Important?   59
How Long Does It Take for Understanding
    to Come?   59
Compass Chart   61
Positive Thinking—An Erroneous
    Concept   63
The Brain as a Computer   65
Using Our Natural State of Mind,
    Rather than Our Thought System   66

9   Contrary to Popular Opinion   69
    Rules   69
    Doing   71
    A Fairy Tale   73
    Service   74
    Selfishness   74
    Intelligence   76
    Patience   77
    Forgiveness   78
    Circumstances   79
    A Horse Story   80
    Seeing What Is without Judgment   81
    Who, Me? I Thought It Was You, It, Them!   82

10   Detours   85
    Insecurity   85
    Judgments   86
    Stereotyping   88
    Judgments from Others   88
    Living for or against Someone Else   89
    Ego and Self-Importance   90

Contents

Self-Centering on Self-Esteem   92
Anger   93
The Past   95
Decisions   98
Lighten Up, Keep It Simple, and Come
   from Love   99
It Gets Easier to Avoid Detours   101

11 Relationships   103
    Separate Realities Relating to Relation-
        ships   104
    Acceptance   108
    Thoughts and Moods Related to
        Relationships   110
    Listening   116
    Have Fun Together   117
    Live in Gratitude   117

12 Myths about Relationships   119
    Myth No. 1: Love Is Blind   119
    Myth No. 2: It Is Important to
        Be Compatible   121
    Myth No. 3: It Is Important to
        Communicate about Problems   123
    Myth No. 4: Never Go to Sleep until
        You Have Resolved an Argument   125
    Myth No. 5: If You Are Not Having Fights
        You Are Not Going "Deep" in Your
        Relationship—or Someone Is Giving in
        Too Much   126
    Myth No. 6: We Will Be Happy When
        Our Circumstances Change   127

Myth No. 7: When You Love Someone, It
Is Natural to Feel Insecure; Jealousy Is
a Sign That You Care   129
Myth No. 8: You Have to Have
a Relationship   133

13 Children   135
Example Is the Best Teacher   136
Feeding Fires   137
In the Beginning   138
Yes or No   139
Listen Deeply   140
Mistakes   141
Recovery   141
Enjoying Children   143

14 Myths of Child Rearing   145
Myth No. 1: Punishment Teaches Children
to Improve Their Behavior   145
Myth No. 2: Children Need to Learn
Obedience   146
Myth No. 3: Be a Parent, Not a Friend,
to Your Children   148
Myth No. 4: Problems Must Be Dealt with
Immediately   149
Myth No. 5: What Other People Think
about Your Parenting Skills Is
Important   149
Myth No. 6: Children Should Be Seen
and Not Heard   151

15 Wisdom, and Lack of Wisdom, from
the Ages   155

If You Can't Say Something Nice,
    Don't Say Anything at All   155
Count to Ten   156
Haste Makes Waste   156
Sticks and Stones Can Break My Bones,
    But Names Will Never Hurt Me   156
A Stitch in Time Saves Nine   157
Idleness Is the Devil's Workshop   157
The Road to Hell Is Paved with
    Good Intentions   159
A Person without Goals Is Like a
    Ship without a Rudder   160
Anything Worth Doing Is Worth
    Doing Well   161
Growth Is Painful   161
It's Too Good to Be True   162
Good Things Always Come to an End   162

16   Keys to Happiness—A Summary   163
    The Principles as Keys to Happiness   164
    Thinking as a Function   164
    Feelings as a Compass   165
    Separate Realities   165
    Mood Levels   165
    Barriers to Happiness   166
    Circumstances   166
    Judgments   166
    Expectations   167
    Assumptions   167
    Beliefs and Realities   168
    Signposts to Happiness   170
    Gratitude   170

Compassion   171
What We See or Feel or Give Is
   What We Get   171
Love and Understanding   172
The Battle between Love and Ego   173
Enjoying What Is While It Is   173
Happiness and Serenity   174

Acknowledgments

I was once a workshop junkie. I used to wonder in jest if I would ever find the last workshop—one that would finally teach me the magic techniques that would give me enough competence and confidence to be truly helpful to myself and others. I never found what I was looking for. Instead, I found something better—principles that taught me where competence, confidence, and wisdom are and always have been—within myself.

The intellectual knowledge that "the kingdom of heaven is within," and "as a man thinketh, so is he" was not new to me, but I had never experienced these truths. I finally discovered a seminar where principles were explained that led me to experience my inner kingdom of happiness and peace of mind. I gratefully acknowledge and give thanks to George Pransky and Robert Kausen, who put up with my "what ifs" and "yes, buts" until I was finally able to hear at a deeper level.

The principles that led to my experience of inner wisdom and serenity have been formulated into a new and revolutionary psychology by Rick Suarez, Ph.D., and Roger C. Mills, Ph.D. These principles, now referred to as The Psychology of Mind,* represent a major breakthrough in the understanding of psychological functioning.

After experiencing such dramatic results in my life from what I learned from George Pransky and Robert Kausen, I felt inspired to spend six months in fellowship at the Advanced Human Studies Institute in Coral Gables, Florida. Studying and working with Dr. Rick Suarez and Dr. Kimberly Kiddoo was truly a beautiful and enriching experience. What a privilege to be led to a deeper understanding of inner resources via the wisdom of these pioneers and innovators in this new psychology.

I originally intended to write this book with Kimberly Kiddoo because she was such an inspiration to me. When she decided not to coauthor the book she encouraged me to use some of her examples because, "Understanding the examples makes them your own, and getting this out in a book will help so many people." I miss her. Dr. Kiddoo is now in private practice in Coral Gables, Florida.

It is with loving appreciation that I acknowledge Dr. William Pettit, a prominent psychiatrist, who dropped his successful practice and position as a national trainer

---

*Rick Suarez, Roger C. Mills, and Darlene Stewart, *Sanity, Insanity, and Common Sense: The Groundbreaking New Approach to Happiness* (New York: Ballantine, Fawcett Columbine, 1987).

of a popular growth seminar when he heard the principles of Psychology of Mind. He moved his family to Florida and was finishing his fellowship at the Advanced Human Studies Institute while I was there. I am filled with gratitude as I remember his delightful influence, which is reflected in this book. Dr. Pettit is now the Director of the Psychiatric Institute of Florida in Bradenton, Florida.

Syd Banks provided the initial inspiration. I am grateful for the opportunities I have had to attend his lectures and experience his wisdom and good feelings. Several people told me that I would get more out of a second reading of his book, *Second Chance,** than I would the first time. I was determined to prove them wrong and fully intended to get everything I could during the first reading. I was delightfully surprised at the profound effect and deeper understanding I experienced when I read *Second Chance* again a few months later.

It was a special thrill to receive an endorsement from Wayne Dyer. His books and tapes have been an inspiration to me and my family for years. His book, *Gifts from Eykis,*† is a special gift for those of us who enjoy laughing while we learn profound truths.

Because my desire was to be instrumental in helping others experience the joy and serenity found in understanding the principles of Psychology of Mind, it has been a gratifying and humbling experience to hear

---

* Syd Banks, *Second Chance* (New York: Ballantine, Fawcett Columbine, 1987).

† Wayne Dyer, *Gifts from Eykis* (New York: Pocket Books, 1983).

from so many people who have read the first edition of *Understanding*. That so many would be touched was beyond my comprehension, and I hope that many more will find serenity through *Understanding*.

It has been a delight working with Mimi McCarty, who has served as editor for this new edition. Anyone who has read the first edition will appreciate her exceptional contribution.

I am especially grateful to my husband, Barry, and my children, to whom this book is dedicated. We continually love and learn from each other. I recently got lost for a short time in feelings of insecurity and was behaving irrationally. My ten-year-old daughter, Mary, later said, "I knew you would soon realize what you were doing, Mom."

1

A Treasure Map

All of us look for answers to help us find happiness and peace of mind. Even though everyone wants this, many find that joy is usually missing from their lives and relationships. Instead, they live in stress, anxiety, dissatisfaction, disappointment, anger, or depression.

An abundance of wisdom about happiness and peace of mind is available through spoken and written words. You may have experienced inspiration by beautiful words of wisdom and vowed *to be better,* and then felt disappointed when you did not maintain those inspired feelings.

Perhaps you have found that sometimes, even when you could remember what you *should do,* you just didn't feel able to do it. You may have had times when you felt like giving in to feelings of discouragement, failure, and self-blame. Then you may have felt

5

inspired to do better again—only to repeat the cycle.

What does it take to *understand* words of wisdom and integrate them into our beings at such a deep level that it becomes natural and easy to live in joy and harmony? How can we remain inspired so that words of wisdom are truly helpful in our lives, instead of becoming more *shoulds* that we feel we can't live up to?

This book reveals ways to live in serenity and happiness by explaining four principles that show you how to access your inner wisdom, common sense, and inspiration—the inner happiness you have heard so much about and have probably occasionally experienced.

We have all heard that happiness is *within,* but many of us do not understand what that means, or we forget and keep looking for happiness outside ourselves. We do not understand the basic principles that allow us to enjoy our inner happiness most of the time.

The four principles of psychological functioning, which can act as a treasure map, have been formulated into the new Psychology of Mind by Rick Suarez, Ph.D., and Roger C. Mills, Ph.D.,* and are discussed in chapters three through six. Once you *understand* these principles you can find the treasures of your natural state of mind—the inner happiness, wisdom, and creative inspiration buried deep within you.

Living in serenity and happiness comes from beautiful feelings inherent within each of us. We learn

---

* Rick Suarez, Roger C. Mills, and Darlene Stewart, *Sanity, Insanity, and Common Sense: The Groundbreaking New Approach to Happiness* (New York: Ballantine, Fawcett Columbine, 1987).

negative processes that keep the natural positive feelings buried. When our inherent good feelings are uncovered we live spontaneously in a happy, loving state of mind. The kingdom of heaven *is* within.

An *understanding* of the four principles is like a treasure map, which can show us how to uncover our natural feelings of peace, love, and joy in living. When these feelings are uncovered, we have easy access to inspiration from our own inner wisdom. And whatever we do from our natural good feelings and inner wisdom will provide joy, ease, and happiness in our lives and relationships.

You may not believe that you have natural good feelings and inherent inner wisdom. That is simply because you are unaware of the negative thoughts and beliefs you have created, and then become enslaved by, which keep you blocked from your natural state of mind. An understanding of the four principles can show you the way back to your natural good feelings.

How can I make such claims? Because an *understanding* of the principles has worked so beautifully in my own life and in the lives of friends, clients, and other therapists who have come to *understand* them. I have watched myself and others find *lasting* peace, joy, and contentment instead of the temporary results experienced when answers are found outside the self.

Words of wisdom that lead to inner happiness now have meaning for me at a deep enough level to make them natural, rather than difficult, to follow. This does not mean I never get *off course* into unhappiness, but the principles show me exactly how I get *off course* and point me back in the direction of my natural good feelings. Like any often-used map, the direction soon becomes so natural that it is easier to find the way without a map, without even thinking about it.

I was once like many therapists who are sincerely motivated to help people, while their own lives are filled with stress, anxiety, dissatisfaction, feelings of inadequacy, depression, or other forms of insecurity. This is not meant as a criticism of therapists. Many of us have been well trained in effective *coping skills,* which can be very helpful, because coping is certainly better than not coping. It brings only temporary relief, however, until the next problem is encountered. Coping is like bailing water when we don't know how to plug the hole in the boat. Bailing is much better than sinking.

The exciting news is that the four basic principles show us how to plug the hole. We don't need to learn how to cope with stress or other forms of insecurity: we can *eliminate* them. This book gives many examples of common *problem situations* in life and relationships that illustrate how the *problem* is eliminated through *understanding.*

Can you imagine what life would be like without problems? I remember being concerned that peace of mind would be boring. What a silly notion! Happiness and peace of mind are great treasures that bring lasting joy. *Understanding* is the *treasure map.*

Someone once asked, "So, what is the point of all this?"

My answer, "To be happy."

Too many people get caught up in other goals and purposes and forget to be happy.

You already know how to be happy, but buried knowledge is unused. This kind of knowledge then seems like a well-kept secret.

I buried my own inner happiness and wisdom for years and lived my life based on illusions of insecurity. This would have surprised many, had they known, because I was very good at achieving all the things people commonly search for in their quest for happiness. Since my search was based on overcoming illusions of insecurity and looking for happiness outside myself, none of my achievements kept me happy for long. My search became more frenetic, and I became a workaholic.

The burden was even heavier because in trying to keep those feelings of insecurity hidden, I needed to *appear* secure to others. It didn't work. The insecure feelings were like quicksand waiting to swallow me every time I *thought* I was failing, or when I rested for very long on my laurels before trying to achieve more *success.*

A client recently said to me, "Well, sure you are happy. Look at all you have."

I replied, "That is the point. I had everything I have now before I learned about these principles, and I still wasn't happy. I paid more attention to my illusions of insecurity and a false need to prove myself than to my natural feelings of gratitude, joy, wisdom, and love. This explains why so many people who have fame, fortune, achievements, or other forms of *success* as defined by our society, are often depressed and unhappy, whereas others who have little are very happy. Happiness has nothing to do with material possessions or achieve-ments. Lasting happiness and peace of mind are found within, no matter what the circumstances."

This treasure map to *understanding* is one of the most valuable gifts I have ever received. It has helped me *see* that I already have everything I need. Much of the time I did not *see* the good feelings and happiness buried deep within myself because I kept looking for happiness outside of myself. I often missed *seeing* what I had because I focused outward instead of enjoying what IS.

I used to be happy about 20 percent of the time. The remainder was spent trying to escape the illusions of insecurity. I am now happy 80 percent of the time, and the 20 percent detours into unhappiness have lost intensity and longevity because I can recognize the thinking that creates my unhappiness. The detour ends when I quit taking those thoughts seriously. The princi-ples taught me to recognize the detours for what they are and to find my way back to sanity.

When I uncovered the natural happiness within myself, I began to truly enjoy and appreciate all that life has to offer—all that I once took for granted. What I once thought I wanted no longer matters. It is impos-sible to feel satisfaction and *want* at the same time.

My life is now based on feelings of security and peace of mind. I now have a compass that lets me know when I get off course and keeps me headed in the direction of deeper *understanding*.

I have found the buried treasure within myself. You can find it too.

HAPPY TREASURE HUNTING!

2

Listening Softly

As you read this book, listen softly. Listen "from your heart," for insight, for a feeling or realization from within that lets you hear truth.

Learning from insight or realization is unlike learning from the intellect. The brain has unlimited capacity and capabilities, but most of us have limited our intellects with a thought system "programmed" with concepts, interpretations, and beliefs. This programmed thought system filters any new possibilities; it tries to fit everything into what it already knows—or rejects it.

Listen softly for a feeling, because words are inadequate to express love, beauty, principle, or any other truth. These intangibles can be understood only through the personal experience of them, which is beyond words. Someone once asked Louis Armstrong to explain jazz. Louis said, "If you can't feel it, I don't know how I can explain it." The only purpose of words in this book is to lead you to the kind of understanding you will feel. If you can't feel it, you will not understand it.

We often focus on words and miss the feeling being expressed. Each person hears words from his or her own frame of reference and interpretation. For example, your mental picture of a dog is different from that of all your friends who loved a different kind of dog. This is why discussions of religion and politics are often avoided; these topics trigger so many differing beliefs and emotions about what is "right" and "wrong" that we stop listening.

Listening softly helps us get past the limitation of words. Words can sound so hollow, whereas the experience of what the words are trying to convey can be so full. The gap between the two is bridged by the understanding that comes from insight. When you listen for a feeling, you will know what is meant in spite of the limitation of words. You will probably even know (from your own inspiration) another way to explain principles of truth that will make more sense to you. And that is the most important thing to understand—*what makes sense to you when you listen to your own wisdom and inspiration.*

Any principle can be difficult to learn, unless we bypass our limited thought system so we can experience *insight.* Conversely, the principles, soon to be explained, help us remember how to bypass our limited thought system. I say remember, because we were born with that capability and used it as children to enjoy life, to learn, and to experience many beautiful things. Insight is a recognition of the obvious. The obvious often eludes us when we are stuck in our programmed thought system.

Remember when you were trying to learn math principles? At first it did not matter how many times you added 2 + 2; it didn't really make sense. Then, suddenly, you *caught on* and could add any combination of numbers. It made sense that 5 + 7 was the same as 7 + 5. This is one example of experiencing insight to understand a principle.

Learning to ride a bicycle is another example. No matter how many times we heard an explanation of balance, it was beyond our comprehension until we experienced balance ourselves.

We kept plugging away at math and practicing balance, even when the principles made no sense to us. We had faith that we would eventually learn and, with these abilities, would be able to produce many good results. Some of us may have practiced out of love for the teacher rather than from faith in future results. Others may have developed a belief that they could not learn and may still have "blocks" about math or balance.

The principles of math and balance do not provide answers. They simply show us how to find answers or how to discover mistakes and make corrections. The principles explained in this book show us how to find answers and make corrections in our lives.

As you read, notice how difficult it can be to *hear* and *understand* the principles when you use your programmed thought system—the intellectual process that blocks inner wisdom and inspiration. You will know you are in touch with your inner wisdom and inspiration when you read something and have that "aha" feeling—or, when you read something you disagree with, instead of getting upset or having negative feelings, you are led to a higher understanding that makes more sense to you than it did before.

You may say with irritation, "But I have heard that before" or "I already know that." When you have "really" heard it at an insight level you do not get irritated at hearing it again. You only feel reaffirmed. The irritation comes from a deep level of knowing that you have not really "heard."

We often hear principles intellectually with just enough understanding to give *lip service*. When we hear at an insight level of understanding or realization, we give *heart service*. The difference between lip service and heart service is the difference between intellectual understanding and life application.

Reading this book could be like putting together a puzzle. Sometimes one piece makes no sense until it fits with another. Perhaps something you read in the middle or at the end will give you the insight to make the beginning more understandable.

This book is short so that it will be easy to read many times. If you get even a glimmer of *insight* the first time, you will get more each subsequent time. Your reading experience will be different as your *understanding* deepens. When your *understanding* is deep enough, it will automatically override your limited, programmed thought system and keep you in touch with your own wisdom.

Most of your questions will be answered as you keep reading. The answers will come not from what you read, but from the insight of your own wisdom and inner understanding. *The purpose of this book is to help you regain greater access to these sources within yourself.*

Understanding is the key to natural happiness and peace of mind.

Listening for a feeling is the key to insight.

Insight is the key to understanding.

This is the cycle. It does not matter where you start. Each aspect leads in the same direction for positive results in your life and relationships.

You are reading this book because you hope to achieve the promised results of eliminating stress and of finding serenity, joy, happiness, and peace of mind. Like math and balance, before understanding, principles can seem complicated. After understanding, they seem beautifully simple. When you catch on to the principles with insight, you will *experience beautiful results in your life.*

Keep listening softly.

3

The Principle of Thinking as a Function

You think! This is the best-kept secret of all. *Understanding* that you think is the key to understanding everything else in life.

You may be saying, "That is not a secret. Everyone knows he or she thinks." Actually, very few people remember that thinking is a function or an ability. Most act like victims of their thoughts, rather than like producers of their thoughts. Instead of knowing that thinking is a function or an ability, they believe that what they think is reality.

Thinking is an ability we use to create our reality; reality is not reflected in our thoughts. Because thoughts come from the inside, and not from the outside, what we think determines what we see—even though we often make the mistake of believing what we see determines what we think. We can think *anything* we choose to think, and our emotions are then a direct result of what we choose to think. Any form of insecurity, stress, or anxiety results from choosing thoughts that produce those kinds of emotions and then believing that those thoughts are *reality* rather than products of our thinking.

For example, try feeling insecure without thinking that you are insecure. It is impossible. *As soon as we take the content of our thoughts seriously, we have forgotten that we think.*

Joe feels inadequate. He believes his inadequacy is real, not recognizing it as just a thought. His inadequacy cannot exist unless he thinks it; but because he believes it is real, he bases his behavior on that thought and acts inadequate.

Melissa believes she is depressed because life is overwhelming. But life cannot be overwhelming; only what she thinks about life makes it feel overwhelming.

Archie Bunker is a bigot. He thinks other people are inferior, and he believes his thoughts are reality, not just thoughts.

People who believe their thoughts are reality have forgotten that they think and that they can think anything they want. They have forgotten that when they change their thoughts, their reality changes.

It is very simple. If you don't like what you are thinking about, stop thinking about it.

You may argue, "How can I possibly stop thinking about what I am thinking about? I tried that, and it didn't work."

You keep thinking certain thoughts only when you believe they are reality and take them seriously. When you stop taking them seriously, it takes effort to keep thinking about them. Understanding the true nature of thinking makes it difficult to take any of your negative thoughts seriously.

Some people go through life with the attitude that life is a celebration—something to enjoy fully. Others have the attitude that life is a chore—something to be endured. There is a very popular poster expressing this negative attitude: "Life is hard, and then you die."

Which is it? A celebration or a chore? The answer depends entirely upon what you think.

Many people argue that attitudes are not a product of thinking, but of circumstances. If attitudes were a product of circumstances, however, it would be impossible to find people who still celebrate life even with terminal cancer or crippling afflictions. But many happy people exist who are experiencing all kinds of supposedly difficult circumstances in life.

We are often touched and inspired by stories of people who swim without arms, ski without legs, "run" races in wheelchairs, start again after "failures," or celebrate life no matter what the circumstances. Conversely, we are often moved to compassion for people who quit celebrating life because they don't realize their thoughts make them more miserable than their circumstances. Understanding the principle of thought as a function does not imply there is a right or wrong way to think. Understanding the principle simply teaches us the many possibilities that come from thinking.

Our understanding goes even deeper when we realize our thinking ability comes from two different sources. One source produces joy and serenity; the other, insecurity and stress.

THINKING FROM A NATURAL STATE OF MIND OR FROM A PROGRAMMED THOUGHT SYSTEM

Each person has a thought system for storing the memories, perceptions, judgments, and beliefs that act like filters, creating his or her unique, separate reality. (The principle of separate realities is discussed in chapter five.)

Each individual also has a natural state of mind through which he or she can experience common sense, wisdom, inspiration, and all the good feelings that are naturally inherent in every human being.

Through our natural state of mind we experience life differently from how we experience life through our thought system. Through our natural state of mind we *see* life freshly, moment to moment with fascination, wisdom, and appreciation. Through our thought system, we see only our beliefs about life, just as Archie Bunker does. When we take thoughts from our thought system seriously, we block our natural state of mind and lose access to our inner wisdom and inspiration. Our natural good feelings cannot get through because they are blocked by the nonsense of our thought system.

We start at an early age to create a thought system, which is made up of our own perceptions and interpretations, as well as the thoughts and interpretations we accept from others. We are very trusting when we are young, usually believing what anyone tells us. Unfortunately, much of what we are told is *nonsense* passed along from generation to generation. This is not done maliciously; our family and friends would not pass on troublesome beliefs if they knew what they were doing. Not knowing any better, they themselves accepted beliefs passed on to them when they were young.

Most of these beliefs are full of "shoulds" and "shouldn'ts" that contain judgments of worth or worthlessness. We are told how we should be in order to be liked and to be successful. We are also told how others should be and how life should be. We, others, and life hardly ever fit these beliefs, so we live with failure, pseudosuccess, anxiety, stress, or disappointment in ourselves, life, and others.

Our thought system also contains helpful information and skills, such as reading, writing, arithmetic, names, and phone numbers, that make life easier and more enjoyable. This information is factual and does not create emotions. We use it for our benefit rather than against ourselves. With understanding we know when it is beneficial to use the stored information in our thought system, and when it is wise to disregard old interpretations and beliefs.

It is the illusionary thoughts, which create negative emotions, that get us into trouble when we believe they are reality. The beliefs and interpretations we accept or create can seem so real that we live and die for them, even when they make no sense.

Senseless thinking is often easier to see in other people than it is to see in ourselves. I remember thinking schizophrenics were really crazy when they thought they saw little green bugs crawling up the wall, or when they believed they were Napoleon. It was obvious to me that those were crazy thoughts. But, of course, all *my* thoughts were serious and real—even the ones that made me miserable.

One psychologist shared with me that before she

21

had a deeper understanding of these principles, she had a client in therapy who believed a garbage truck was going to eat her.

The psychologist spontaneously laughed and said, "That is a silly thought." She had spoken from her common sense and wisdom, but felt a little embarrassed because she had been taught that it is inappropriate to laugh at something a client is taking seriously. Fortunately, the client *heard* the truth of those words at an even deeper level than they had been spoken, and she began to improve significantly. Several months later the psychologist asked what had made the difference in her recovery.

The client replied, "It was the day you told me my thoughts couldn't hurt me."

We all have silly thoughts we take seriously. Yet when we know they are just thoughts, they can't hurt us. Instead of living as though our thoughts have power over us, we will remember that we have power over them, and the negative thoughts will lose their power to make our lives miserable.

Another client quit having panic attacks after hearing the above story. She said, "The last time a panic attack started, I knew it was just my thoughts. I laughed and felt fine."

I know it is not this simple for everyone. It wasn't for me. Some people *understand* sooner than others.

No one wants the misery created by negative thoughts. Some people seem to live as if they do, only because they do not understand the difference between thinking through their natural state of mind and thinking through their programmed thought system.

The next time you feel upset or miserable, notice what you are thinking. Your emotions are created by your thoughts. Taking your negative thoughts seriously simply means you have forgotten you created them in the first place. Or, you may be believing as reality the thoughts others have created and passed on to you.

When we *realize* that thinking is a function or an ability rather than a reality, we can easily dismiss the negative thoughts we create and live from our natural state of mind to express our inherent good feelings. The first thing our inner wisdom helps us realize is how funny it is to take negative thoughts seriously and base our lives on them.

Many have argued, "Good feelings are not natural to me. It is more natural for me to feel stressed or depressed. I don't try to feel these things; they are just naturally there." They are not just naturally there. There is a negative thought behind every negative feeling.

Can you imagine the problems babies and young children would have if they tried to learn to walk and talk through insecurities produced by a programmed thought system? What would happen if they formed beliefs about falling such as, "Oh dear, I failed again. I am not a very good person. I had better not try again, or I might fall again, and then what would people think?"

When we rediscover that childlike quality of not thinking through a programmed thought system, our life becomes as much fun as a child's. We lose all forms of insecurity, and each day is full of wonder, adventure, and delight in all there is to experience in life.

If it seems that I am going on and on about this principle, it is because I know this can be the most difficult one to understand. Most people try to figure it out from their programmed thought system. The filters of the thought system created the distortions in the first place, so it is impossible to see things differently while using that same thought system. Thus, I am saying the same thing over and over in different ways, hoping that one of the ways will sneak past your filters and reach your inner wisdom and common sense, where all great discoveries and new learning take place.

Looking at life through our programmed thought system is the same as looking at the world through ***extremely dark*** glasses labeled judgment, blame, expectations, pride, ego, anger, shoulds, and other forms of insecurity based on thought. These glasses are like blinders and filters that distort our view of life. The distortion becomes our reality and shuts out everything else, including the truth. Are you wondering, "What is the truth?"

The truth is what you *see* when you take off the dark glasses (dismiss negative thoughts). Have you ever noticed how different everything looks when you replace judgment with compassion, complaints with gratitude, hate with love? Whenever we have any negative feelings, we can recognize that we are wearing one of our pairs of ugly dark glasses (our thought system). As soon as we take them off (dismiss our thoughts), we *see* from the perspective of our natural state of mind, and our reality changes.

Sometimes you may be aware that you are looking at the world through those dark glasses, but you can't seem to drop them because they feel stuck on with super glue. It may seem as if you are "stuck in your thought system." Knowing what is happening, even when we can't seem to get out of it, shortens the "stuckness" tremendously. It is only *thinking* about our stuckness, and taking it seriously, that allows it to hang on and get worse. It helps simply to realize what is happening and wait for it to pass rather than to worry about it.

When first learning about thought, many people find themselves in variations of the following states of thought.

STATES OF THOUGHT

1. Being caught up in thoughts and *taking them seriously.*
2. Being caught up in thoughts, but not taking them quite as seriously because of an *understanding* that they are just thoughts.
3. Being at rest. Dismissing thoughts and getting quiet to wait for inspiration and insight from our natural state of mind.
4. Inspiration—when our natural state of mind is expressing wisdom and common sense.

We are usually in several variations of these states of thought throughout the day. *Understanding* the principles simply lets us know what is happening, and thus shortens the visits to states one and two.

When we understand our programmed thought system for the filter that it is, we will be able to bypass it, except for occasional, short visits. When we understand what happens when we are there, we won't want to stay for long. Each visit will simply confirm that thinking through our thought system does not produce happiness and peace of mind (unless we are using it to remember useful facts and skills).

Eykis points out in *Gifts from Eykis,* "Thinking is the basis for every single major and minor difficulty you encounter. The problems that arise in politics, religion, education, families, business, the military, society, medicine, and every form of human enterprise are due to self-programed unreal thinking." *

At this point or sooner, many people get the notion that thinking is "the bad guy," and we should not think. Thinking is a beautiful gift through which we experience the beauty of life. Insights from our natural state of mind can be experienced only through the function of thinking.

The key is understanding where thoughts originate. When they originate in our thought system we usually do not experience peace of mind and satisfaction. We experience serenity when thoughts are the means we use to experience the wisdom, inspiration, and inherent good feelings that flow from our natural state of mind.

We are almost always thinking. *Understanding* makes it natural to dismiss negative thoughts which come from our programmed thought system and to enjoy a nice life naturally.

The following principle gives us the key to know where our thoughts are coming from.

---

* Wayne Dyer, *Gifts from Eykis,* pp. 118–119 (New York: Pocket Books, 1983).

4

The Principle of Feelings as a Compass

Our feelings are like a compass, letting us know where we are on our treasure map. When we feel good, we are on the right course, through our natural state of mind, to find happiness and peace of mind in life. When we feel bad, we are off course into our thought system. Remember, it is impossible to have negative feelings without thoughts from your thought system. Thus, negative feelings are the compass that lets us know we are thinking from our thought system.

Negative feelings tell us it is time to dismiss negative thoughts. Positive feelings tell us we are experiencing life through our natural state of mind, where we have access to our inherent good feelings.

Many people do not believe that good feelings are inherent. They are. Good feelings are like corks in water, naturally bobbing to the surface unless weighted down. Good feelings are natural in human beings unless they are weighted down with seriously taken negative thoughts. Most of us, however, have become adept at taking our thoughts seriously.

While first learning about the principles, I thought *understanding* meant I would never again "get lost" in my thought system, even for a short time, and I became very disappointed in myself whenever I took my thoughts seriously.

I had an insightful experience when my inner wisdom let me know it did not matter that my negative thoughts kept creeping in. (They were not actually "creeping" in. We become so proficient at instantaneously pulling up "files" from our programmed thought system that we forget they are still our moment-to-moment creations. It then seems that thoughts creep into our mind beyond our control, which is impossible.) After this realization, I experienced just "watching" those thoughts without judging them. I even felt a tolerant affection for my negative thoughts. When I understood they were just thoughts, they could not hurt me. It was easy to laugh and dismiss them.

Everyone gets off course—some of us more often than others. *Understanding* helps us not to take getting off course seriously, not to judge ourselves, and to be open for the inspiration that leads us back on course.

A word of caution: Many people claim they are just following their *feelings* when they do negative things, like "getting out" their anger, or telling another person that their judgments about them are "the truth."

Any feelings that are negative or produce negative results come from a distorted frame of reference or programmed thought system. The feelings that come from our natural state of mind are compassion, gratitude, humor, understanding, and love.

Positive feelings flow naturally from our natural state of mind. The *feeling* comes first and is then experienced through the gift of thinking. Negative feelings are experienced after we create negative thoughts from our thought system. In other words, *if the feeling comes first, it is from your natural state of mind; if the feeling comes second, it is from your thought system.*

Soon after hearing this, I had an opportunity to experience the truth of it. During a one-week seminar in which I was learning more about the principles, I called home to see how my children were doing. I was informed that my thirteen-year-old son had been suspended from school. This is how he told the story:

"I found some cigarettes in my locker. I don't know how they got there. I was just putting them in my pocket to take them to the principal when a teacher came by and took me to the principal."

My thoughts went crazy for a few minutes. "He is lying to us. I'm a failure as a mother. If he is smoking cigarettes, he is probably also using alcohol and drugs. He is going to ruin his life. What will people think?" I was feeling pretty upset, so my feeling compass let me know loud and clear that I was caught up in my thought system and was not seeing things clearly. I dismissed my compass instead of my thoughts for a minute and used more thoughts to argue with my inner wisdom. "Yes, but this is different. These are really terrible circumstances over which I have no control. How could I possibly see them differently? I am going to have to scold him severely, 'ground' him for at least a month,

29

take away all his privileges, and let him know he is ruining his life."

Fortunately, I had too much faith in the principles to take those thoughts seriously. I dismissed my crazy thoughts, and inspiration quickly surfaced. I then *saw* the circumstances in a completely different way and felt understanding and compassion for my son's view of the situation. He had just entered junior high school, where the pressure is enormous to follow the crowd rather than to follow common sense.

When I got home I listened to my inspiration and knew what to do. I sat down with my son, put my arm around him, and said, "I'll bet it's tough trying to figure out how to say no to your friends so you won't be called a nerd or a party pooper." He had been expecting my usual craziness and hardly knew how to respond to my sanity.

He tentatively said, "Yeah."

I went on, "And I'll bet the only reason you would ever lie to us is because you love us so much you don't want to disappoint us." Tears filled his eyes, and he gave me a big hug. I responded with tears in my own eyes as we experienced those wonderful feelings of mutual love. I reassured him, "If you think you could ever disappoint us enough to diminish our love, then we are not doing a good enough job of letting you know how much we love you, unconditionally."

We can only guess what the results would have been had I followed my crazy thoughts to interact with my son. My guess is that my craziness would have inspired increased rebelliousness instead of increased closeness.

I am continually grateful for the principle of using my feelings as a compass to let me know when I am "off track." Whenever I feel upset, angry, judgmental, disappointed, or any other negative emotion, I know my feelings are being created by thoughts I am taking seriously. As soon as I recognize that and dismiss the thoughts, I am filled with natural good feelings.

Dismissing negative thoughts is not the same as sticking your head in the sand. Instead, it is like taking off blinders and filters so you can see the situation with perspective. Sometimes the problem disappears along with the negative thoughts. Other times the problem may still be there, but it looks and feels different. You will see solutions rather than problems, because from a natural state of mind solutions are obvious. It is amazing how different the world seems when you dismiss negative thoughts so your natural good feelings can surface. Common sense and wisdom flow.

5

The Principle of Separate Realities

Another well-kept secret is the fact that everyone lives in a separate reality. This simply means that we all *interpret* things differently.

You may object again, "That is not a secret. Everyone knows that." It is true that most of us have heard this principle, but we forget to apply it in our lives. A popular example often used to explain the principle of separate realities is that everyone who sees an accident describes it differently. The reason becomes obvious when we *understand* that everyone sees through the filters of his or her own unique thought system.

We have separate realities because everyone has a different thought system made up of unique memories, interpretations, and beliefs that act like filters through which present events are seen. When we view the world through these filters it is impossible to see what *IS* with fresh perspective.

Hearing about separate realities, however, and understanding the principle at a deep level are not the same. When we really *understand* the fact of separate realities, we will stop spending so much time and energy trying to change the reality of others. Remember, there is a difference between understanding from an intellectual level (rendering lip service) and understanding from an insight level (offering heart service).

Without *understanding* we are unaware of our filters, and we therefore think our interpretations are real. We become convinced that if we try hard enough we can persuade others that our reality is the *right* one. This NEVER WORKS—so nations go to war, marriages break up, and parents and children experience a "generation gap." The reverse can also apply. Some people think their reality is wrong, or is not as good as others'. They spend a lot of time feeling inadequate, insecure, and depressed.

When we don't understand separate realities, we have thoughts like, "How could they possibly be like that or do that? They would be happier if they did it my way, liked my kind of music (especially at the volume I prefer), ate the foods I like, and loaded the dishwasher the way I do."

We usually understand separate realities when visiting another country. We could not enjoy traveling if we told people of other countries they should speak our language and change all their customs. Traveling is enjoyable when we learn all we can about differences and find them fascinating.

Phil and Lisa experienced separate realities soon after they were married. Phil was an "early bird"; he loved getting up at dawn full of energy and ready to enjoy the day. Every morning he bounded out of bed and sang loudly in the shower, hoping Lisa would wake up. Noticing her still in bed with the covers pulled over her head, he would noisily bounce on the bed as he put on his shoes and socks, thinking, "If she really loved me, she would get up and enjoy this time with me."

Lisa, totally annoyed at what she saw as "his inconsiderateness," would be thinking, "If he really loved me, he would know I hate getting up early and would be quiet and let me sleep."

They often discussed their differences, but neither really "heard" the other because each was more interested in changing, than in understanding, the other. They both felt like they were talking to a wall as they tried to make their points. What they did not realize is that they were talking to two walls—the wall of their own reality as well as the wall of the other's reality.

Christmases were a disaster. When Lisa was growing up, everyone in her family had received one very nice, expensive present for Christmas. In Phil's family everyone had enjoyed the fun of opening a lot of inexpensive presents. So Lisa would buy Phil one nice, expensive present, and Phil would buy Lisa a lot of inexpensive presents. Every Christmas they felt disappointed and misunderstood, each thinking the other was too dense to know how to *really* enjoy Christmas.

We can laugh at Phil and Lisa's foolishness in not seeing how simply they could solve their problems by respecting their separate realities instead of by trying to change each other. Nonetheless, when dealing with our own precious beliefs, we often become just as blind.

Have you noticed how important it "seems" to tell

others, especially those we love, when we think they are "wrong"? Then we wonder why they don't appreciate it.

Bill used to dread visiting his father because they both always ended up with bad feelings. Bill shared, "We used to spend all our time together arguing about who was right and who was wrong. I was certainly never going to admit I was wrong, because it seemed very clear to me that I wasn't. Dad would not admit he was wrong, even though I made every effort to let him know how old-fashioned his ideas were. Understanding separate realities was a godsend for me. Dad and I no longer argue over our differences. I respect how he sees things and know I would see them the same way if I were in his shoes. Now we just share the love and gratitude we have and enjoy each other's company."

Nor is it helpful to judge your own reality. One day when I was judging myself for not having a deeper *understanding* of the principles, I suddenly *realized* that any form of judgment would only block my understanding. When I stopped judging my present reality, I could *see* that to say I should be farther along than I am, or that someone else should have a different reality than they do, makes as much sense as saying a rosebud should be a rose in full bloom.

Every human being is in the process of evolving, learning, and changing in awareness of what life is all about. Getting in the way with our judgments only creates negativity and impedes progress. Can you imagine how much more helpful we would be to ourselves and others if we were loving and compassionate instead of judgmental?

A master gardener does not fret because his or her roses are not growing into petunias, but simply nurtures all of the flowers with water, weeding, and fertilizer so they can reach their full potential as roses, petunias, begonias, or whatever they are. We can likewise simply enjoy and nurture who we and others are rather than destroy our natural capacity to enjoy a beautiful life uncorrupted with "shoulds" and "oughts."

Shoulds are not necessary when we have access to wisdom. If we are truly happy we could not do anything to hurt others or ourselves. Nurturing ourselves and others comes naturally when we have *understanding*. Wisdom lets us know that *the key is not to judge, but to love and nurture.*

Our world expands greatly when we *understand* and appreciate separate realities. It is then possible to enjoy differences (or at least understand them) instead of fighting over them. When we quit seeing separate realities as right or wrong, we see ourselves and others without judgment. This leaves us without all those negative feelings we are stuck with when we are being judgmental. People who insist they must be judgmental to keep the world from going to "hell," find they live most of their life in "hell," which does not help the world.

"But some things really are wrong!" you may argue. With *understanding* we see that this need not be an issue, because everyone does the best he or she can with what he or she knows. When we see the innocence in all behavior and feel compassion or interest, instead of judgment, we are much happier. And when we have *understanding* it is natural to "forgive them, for they know not what they do."

If your thought system is resisting, you are probably dredging up the worst possible examples you can imagine, such as murder, rape, and burglary. Self-righteousness, hatred, or any form of negative judgment only contaminates your common-sense judgment that arises from your inner wisdom and that leads to positive action. You then become like the thing or person you judge or hate, spreading more negativity in the world. When you live in your natural state of mind you will know what to do about these issues to get the best possible results. You will "act" from love and wisdom.

Higher levels of understanding will come naturally from the positive feelings that surface when judgmental thoughts about separate realities are dismissed.

6

The Principle of Mood Levels, or Levels of Consciousness

Everyone has moods. Some people *seem* to fluctuate between mood extremes more than others, but we all experience times when we feel good and times when we feel low. Have you noticed how different your own *separate reality* is, depending on whether your mood is high or low? When you are in a high mood, you *see* things one way; when you are in a low mood, you *see* the same things differently.

For example, recall those times when you were driving along in a good mood and someone needed to cut in front of you, and you cheerfully waved them in, remembering all the times you have been in the same situation. Now, recall the times you were in a low mood and you stepped on the gas, determined not to let them in, mumbling about how stupid and inconsiderate *they* were. When we are in a low mood everything looks bad. We may feel overwhelmed and have feelings of impending doom, and there seems to be no way out.

Higher moods or levels of consciousness simply mean that we can see things with more perspective and with greater understanding of the *big picture* because we are living in our natural state of mind. Lower moods or levels of consciousness simply mean that we have lost perspective and understanding because we are living in our thought system.

Reality is greatly distorted with lost perspective. The distortion is heavily sprinkled with ego, expectations, and judgments. At a time of lost perspective, however, our distorted thoughts seem like the only possibility.

Often we are unaware of the thoughts that have created our low mood, and trying to figure out the cause usually makes things worse. The secret is knowing that moods are not nearly as bad as the thoughts we have about them; it is our thoughts about low moods that can make them seem really awful. The key is to patiently wait for the mood to pass.

I remember when I used to get depressed. Feeling inadequate and insecure about something, I would retreat into depression. Then I would be upset with myself for being depressed, thereby feeling more inadequate and insecure and getting more depressed. I did not understand the vicious cycle I was creating with my thoughts. Later, I started looking forward to my depressions because I used them as an excuse to lie in bed all day and read. My depressions quit lasting very long when I started enjoying them. I finally saw the obvious and realized I did not have to get depressed in order to take a day to rest and enjoy myself. I could simply follow my common sense, which was letting me know it was time to get quiet.

A quiet mind is the best cure for a low mood. You have a quiet mind naturally when you dismiss thoughts from your thought system. Sometimes the simple realization that "it is just a mood," will be enough to immediately raise your level of consciousness. The moment this happens your thoughts will be dismissed, and you will have access to inner wisdom, common sense, and inspiration, enabling you to see things from a different perspective. Your reality will change.

Ellen was upset because a department store had failed to refund her money as promised. She took out her anger on the customer service clerk, who reacted by being rude to Ellen. As soon as Ellen realized what was happening her mood shifted so she saw things differently. She then said to the clerk, "You really have a tough job, don't you?"

The clerk responded immediately, in a better mood, "I sure do." From then on she was very helpful, and the problem was easily solved.

It all goes back to thought. In lower levels of consciousness we *react* from a thought system full of negativity. In higher levels of consciousness we *act* from inspiration, common sense, and wisdom.

It is impossible to see anything with perspective when we are in a low mood. As soon as we see with perspective, our mood changes. It makes no sense to trust any thoughts or feelings we have in a low state of consciousness because they are being filtered through our programmed thought system rather than coming from wisdom and common sense. *Understanding* this principle teaches us to *get quiet* (verbally, physically, and mentally) when we are at a low level, and wait for it to pass.

NOW YOU SEE IT; NOW YOU DON'T

High or low levels of consciousness are not a matter for value or moral judgment. Consciousness is a state of awareness, perspective, or insight. Sometimes we *see* it, and sometimes we don't. The moment we recognize that we are seeing things from a lower level of consciousness, we have jumped to a higher level of consciousness. It takes perspective to realize we are not seeing something with perspective. So, the moment we recognize we have not been SEEING clearly, we are *seeing* clearly. However, if in the next moment we judge ourselves because we didn't see clearly initially, we have lost our perspective again.

When we are in a higher level of consciousness we feel love, understanding, compassion, forgiveness, and gratitude. We feel satisfaction and peace of mind. We see things with greater understanding and perspective. We do not have to try to make ourselves feel these things through positive thinking. In a higher level of consciousness we naturally feel them.

I can hear your question, "Yes, but what about all those times when I am not in a good mood or at a higher level of consciousness? How do I get out of my low mood if I don't try to figure it out or use positive thinking?"

Feeling low happens, just like storms. We don't try to figure out how to stop a storm, or why it is there, or how to change it. We simply do whatever is necessary to minimize damage, make ourselves as comfortable as possible, and wait for the storm to pass.

A sailor knows the importance of dropping the sails when coming into a storm. With *understanding* we know the importance of dropping negative thoughts when we are in a low mood or have any negative feelings.

Low moods can change immediately with recognition, or they can be something like the flu, hanging around even when we know what they are. When we get the flu, we know that the best thing to do is to take care of ourselves until it passes; we are also careful not to spread it around. It is wise to treat your low moods in the same way; take care of yourself and don't spread them around.

GRATITUDE

I have found that one of the quickest ways to change my mood is through gratitude. It is difficult to hang on to silly thoughts while appreciating all there is to be grateful for. Once I was in such a sour mood I couldn't think of anything to be grateful for. Then I looked down at my hands and was struck by the absolute miracle of my ability to move my fingers. Then I looked up and saw the sky. How beautiful! Love, beauty, and miracles are all around us whenever we are willing to be aware.

Sue Pettit had a wonderful insight about moods and thoughts and was inspired to write a poem entitled

"Lily's Loose."* Notice the similarity of Lily Tomlin's role as Ernestine at the switchboard and what happens when we let our thought system take over.

Lily's Loose

Lily is the operator at the switchboard of my brain.
And when she starts reacting, my life
    becomes insane.
She's supposed to be employed by me—and play a
    passive role.
But anytime I'm insecure—Lily takes control.

Lily's loose, Lily's loose, Lily's loose today.
Tell everyone around me just to clear out of
    my way.
The things I say won't make much sense—all
    COMMON SENSE is lost.
'Cause when Lily's at the switchboard—my wires
    all get crossed.

Lily is my own creation, thought I needed
    her with me
To organize and then recall all my life's history.
But she started taking liberty with all
    my information.
And whenever she starts plugging in—I get a
    bad sensation.

---

* "Lily's Loose" and many other wonderful poems, which beautifully and humorously illustrate the principles of Psychology of Mind, are available in a book entitled *Coming Home* by Sue Pettit, published by Sunrise Press, Fair Oaks, CA (1-800-456-7770).

Lily's Loose, Lily's Loose, Lily's loose today.
Tell all my friends and relatives to clear out
   of my way.
I don't give hugs and kisses when I'm in this
   frame of mind.
And please don't take me seriously—it'd be a
   waste of time.

She looks out through my eyeballs and sees
   what I do see.
Then hooks up wires to my past—she thinks
   she's helping me!
When I'm in a good mood, I can smile at
   her endeavor.
But when I'm in a bad mood—Lily's boss, and
   is she clever.

Lily's loose, Lily's loose, Lily's loose today.
Tell the world to hurry by and stay out
   of my way.
I'm feeling very scattered—I'm lost in
   my emotion.
Lily's on a rampage, and she's causing
   a commotion.

Understanding what low moods are makes it natural and obvious to get quiet and wait for them to pass—or to know enough not to spread our bad moods around—or to forgive ourselves and others when we don't have enough understanding to snap out of it or wait for it to pass. *There are many levels of understanding.*

7

What Now?

Many people become frightened or annoyed when they first hear these principles. Because they habitually use their thought systems to try to figure things out, they can't imagine solving problems any other way. They are also used to blaming circumstances as the cause of their thinking rather than realizing it is their thinking about circumstances that creates their feelings.

Others misinterpret the principles to mean they should quit thinking and become a blob. The opposite is true. Once we truly *understand* the principles, we stop being slaves to our thought systems, and thinking becomes our servant. When we become slaves to our thought system we lack access to our inner wisdom, thus limiting our perspective and awareness of unlimited possibilities.

We rarely stop thinking, even in our sleep. The

point is not to stop thinking; it is to understand that *thinking is a function* and that we have the ability to think anything we want to. *Understanding* helps us know when our thoughts are coming from a limited, distorted thought system, and when our thoughts are the formulation of inspiration, common sense, and wisdom from our natural state of mind.

Understanding brings unlimited freedom; we need no longer be prisoners to our programmed beliefs and negativity. On the other hand, a misunderstanding of the principles can lead to misuse. I often hear comments like the following:

"I'm afraid to ask a question, or people will know I'm not very 'high in consciousness.'"

"I still have negative thoughts, so I must not understand a thing."

"I'm a failure because I yelled at my children. I lost my patience and forgot to see the insecurity behind their behavior."

"I really thought I understood and would not get 'caught up' in my thought system again. The very next day I let myself get hooked into negativity, just like Pavlov's dog. I felt very discouraged and disappointed in myself."

"I just can't feel compassion when my wife drinks, or my husband yells at me, or a friend disappoints me, or things don't turn out the way I want them to. I get angry or upset."

These comments indicate a lack of deeper *understanding,* but it is not helpful to add negative judgment. When we first learn math principles, we make mistakes. As our *understanding* grows, we make fewer mistakes

48

or use our understanding to correct the mistakes. *"Negative judgment only hampers the good feelings that encourage learning."* We can enjoy mistakes when we realize they are simply part of our learning experience. We can enjoy being a rosebud until we become a rose in full bloom.

I once mistakenly believed that if the principles were true, I would be perfect all the time. With *understanding,* the concepts of "perfect" and "mistakes" are totally different. Whenever we get upset about mistakes or "not being perfect," we are ego-involved. This simply means we have a *belief* that our self-worth is dependent upon being a certain way or having others be a certain way. Our expectations do not allow for mistakes. How silly! Life is full of *"making mistakes,"* if that is how you want to label some of the things we do.

Fortunately, children have no concept of *mistake* when they fall down while learning to walk. They don't waste any time thinking about their fall. If they get hurt they may cry for a few minutes before forgetting about it and going on. Understanding the principles helps us recapture that childlike innocence and state of mind.

Edison was once chided, "It is too bad you had so many failures before you were successful."

Edison replied, "I didn't have any failures. I learned many things that did not work."

By simply giving us a direction or a point of reference on our treasure map, principles are like natural laws. The natural law of gravity includes no rule that you *should* not jump off a building; it simply explains what happens if you do. Similarly, the principle of thought as a function includes no rule that you should not think from your thought system; it simply explains what happens if you do.

Making mistakes in math is not disastrous. It does not even seem like a bother to go back over our figures to find the mistakes and correct them when we are feeling gratitude for the knowledge allowing us to do that. Knowing how to correct mistakes is simply part of the principle. And, for some of us, not knowing how to use calculus does not mean we cannot use addition to make our lives easier. Not having a deeper understanding of the principles does not keep us from experiencing the benefits of what we do know.

Although airplanes are usually slightly off course more than they are exactly on course, pilots do not waste time feeling upset about being off course, but simply use the principles of navigation to keep getting back on course.

Recently I had thoughts that produced feelings of inadequacy. I found myself wondering, "Will these people like me? Why would they want to spend any time with me?" In the past I would have taken those thoughts seriously and either withdrawn, pretending I didn't care, or tried to show off in some way to *make* them like me. I noticed the thoughts, dismissed them, and enjoyed myself with those inherent good feelings that surfaced. Next time I may act on thoughts of inadequacy and not enjoy myself.

The principles let me know when I am on course (because I feel great) and when I am off course (because I feel bad). When I am able to dismiss the content of my thinking, I feel grateful. When I do not drop these thoughts, I continue to feel bad.

My present level of understanding has increased the amount of time I feel great. I would be foolish to believe the principles are invalid because my understanding is not yet deep enough that I never have a negative thought. It is deep enough that I do not take those thoughts as seriously as I used to, even when I am taking them seriously enough to disturb my peace at all.

When we get *caught up* in our thought system, it is not helpful to feel guilt or blame or failure. It is helpful simply to know what is happening. Gratitude for that knowledge will be enough to help us get quiet and make room for inspiration, and then we can watch the magic happen.

It is helpful neither to fight our thoughts, nor to try to control them. This is like fighting a whirlpool or trying to control it. If we fight and struggle when we get caught in a whirlpool, we will drown; if we relax and get very quiet, it will carry us down, spitting us out the bottom so we can float to the surface. Understanding makes the difference. Anyone who did not know about a whirlpool would probably become fearful and fight it. Even knowing the importance of relaxing and waiting for the whirlpool to spit us out the bottom, we might still find it difficult to do. A person would need a lot of faith to relax in a whirlpool before having the experience of its working, but anyone who had this information from a reliable source (someone who has had the experience) would be very foolish indeed to fight the whirlpool.

Fighting thoughts that make you unhappy is not a life-and-death matter; it is just a matter of happiness or unhappiness. If you want happiness, it might take faith to follow suggestions from others who understand the principles that lead to happiness. Once you experience results for yourself, you won't need to rely on anyone else's wisdom because you will have access to your own wisdom and inspiration.

If you are still struggling with these ideas, you are probably trying to understand the principles from your thought system. Your reading this far indicates that your inner wisdom is also *hearing,* in spite of your thoughts. *Understanding* will come from your hidden wisdom when you least expect it. Not expecting it means you have quit thinking about it (quit struggling) so that your inner wisdom and inspiration can surface.

Confusion can be a good sign of progress; it can mean your thought system is being scrambled. This is a good time to drop thought and stop trying to figure it out, leaving room for inspiration.

QUIET

Quiet is not necessarily an absence of action, but an absence of negative thoughts running wild in a thought system that takes them seriously. True quiet is not something to do; IT IS A FEELING.

Before *understanding,* it makes sense to get quiet (in the sense of something to do), because slowing down can make it easier to listen for a feeling and to be more open to insight. With *understanding,* quiet is natural.

Quiet is the feeling we have when we dismiss negative thoughts. If negative thoughts were inspiring frenetic activity *to prove something,* then that activity will also be dismissed, and we will *feel* and *be* more quiet.

Being quiet does not mean sacrificing productivity; instead, we will simply be more selective in what we want to produce. We will also be much more efficient when negative thoughts are not interfering and blinding us to the obvious.

Quiet is the humility we feel in the absence of negative thoughts and beliefs. In this quiet and humble state of mind we have access to our inner wisdom and inspiration.

True quiet is total humility.

SO WHAT? BIG DEAL! WHO SAYS?

How many people live their lives making a big deal out of crazy thinking, whether it comes from their own thought system or the thought systems of others. *Understanding* the principles helps us see the humor in making such a big deal out of silly thoughts.

Understanding levels of consciousness makes it natural to stop taking low moods and negative thinking seriously, allowing good feelings to surface.

Understanding separate realities makes it natural to feel compassion or interest rather than judgment.

Understanding that thinking is a function makes it natural to dismiss negative thoughts, allowing inspiration from our inner wisdom and common sense to be available.

Using our feelings as a compass lets us know when we have momentarily forgotten our understanding.

The principles explain the question of "who says?" *Understanding* helps us to question beliefs and suggestions from our own thought system and from others', so that we gain confidence in our own wisdom and common sense. Following our common sense and wisdom, we will know what to do to create joy and ease in our lives, and wonderful relationships with others.

SUGGESTIONS

It doesn't matter if you follow any of the suggestions proposed in this book, because their only purpose is to help you see the principles. If you don't *see* the wisdom behind the suggestions, they will only be seen as more "rules" and "shoulds" and will create more insecurity, rebellion, argument, or some other kind of dissatisfaction. If a suggestion doesn't inspire insight from your inner wisdom, forget about it. Don't *think* about it; just keep *listening* from your heart, and insight will creep up on you when you least expect it.

Suggestions about what "to do" will be meaningful only if you *see* for yourself the wisdom behind the suggestion. If you *see* the wisdom, the suggestions will trigger your own insight and inspiration. You will feel something like, "Of course! That makes sense."

Insight means you have captured the feeling rather than the words. That feeling may lead you to follow the suggestion or to do something much different. You will then be well on your way, because no one knows how to solve your problems better than you do when you are following your inner wisdom, common sense, and inspiration. The whole point of this book is to help you know that.

Your inherent good feelings from your natural state of mind will guide you in what to do for positive results.

Follow the direction of your inner good feelings, and
what to do will be obvious.

Thought

I'm thinking
   thoughts from long ago.
I'm thinking
   tomorrow, what may be so.
I forget I'm thinking.
It's not thought
   this is real.
I forget what I think
   determines how I feel.

I'm missing
   life before my eyes.
I'm missing
   beauty
      in favor of lies.

What I see is me.
I thought it was you.
The observed exists only
   in the eyes of the observer's view.
The pot calls the kettle black
   for only blackness sees black.

I realized I'm thinking.
   I laugh
      and life is beautiful.

8

What Thoughts Are You Willing to Give Up Your Happiness For?

One day I put a nice oak table in the garage for storage. Other family members started putting their junk (treasures to them) on the table. I complained, nagging, "Don't put your things on the oak table or it will get scratched." No one listened, and everything from tools and bicycle parts to a worn-out car battery ended up on the table.

Finally, I went into the garage and cleaned off all the junk so I could cover the table with something to protect it. Sure enough, it was scratched and gouged.

I was angry! Fortunately I had some errands to do, so no one had to listen to me. I drove around, totally lost in my negative thoughts—taking them very seriously.

My feelings let me know that my anger was making me feel upset and miserable. As soon as I became aware of what I was doing to myself with my thoughts, my mood changed. I had to laugh as I began to *see* things differently.

From our natural state of mind we usually have a wonderful sense of humor. I realized my family had not been irresponsible for putting things on the table; I had been irresponsible by not protecting it in the first place.

Then my insight let me see that I was living my life for scratches in an oak table when there were so many other, much nicer possibilities. It was a beautiful day, and I had been missing it. I had so many things to be grateful for, and I was taking them all for granted. A question came from my inner wisdom, *"What thoughts are you willing to give up your happiness for?"*

Everyone who hears this story thinks it is funny that I didn't see the obvious from the beginning and have enough sense to cover the table in the first place. This is the point. Craziness is usually obvious to anyone who is not "caught up" in it. When we are caught up in a certain way of interpreting the world, it seems like the only possible reality.

When we are angry, all we *see* is a world full of bitterness. When we are loving, we see a world of love, compassion, understanding, forgiveness, beauty, gratitude, satisfaction, and peace of mind.

Happiness and beauty are always right in front of our eyes, yet we often cover up our natural good feelings with negative thoughts. Negative thoughts create negative emotions, which shut out the beauty of life.

We then miss so much. *WHAT WE THINK IS WHAT WE GET!*

WHICH PRINCIPLE IS THE MOST IMPORTANT?

The principles are all interrelated, and any one can come first. Sometimes we will see beauty everywhere because we are in a *good mood* or at a *high level of consciousness.* Other times, when we are "caught up in negative thinking," remembering that *thoughts are just thoughts* will raise our level of consciousness so we *see* things differently.

Sometimes, when we think we are *right* about something, remembering the *fact of separate realities* may create humility, and we will then *see* different realities as interesting rather than as right or wrong. Another time, we may use our *feelings as a compass* to let us know we are off track. That alone may raise our mood level, or we may know we need to *get quiet until understanding comes from inspiration.*

HOW LONG DOES IT TAKE FOR UNDERSTANDING TO COME?

Sometimes understanding comes in an instant; sometimes it takes longer.

Syd Banks, philosopher and author of *Second Chance,** received instant *understanding* from one statement, which he *heard.* He was walking along the

---

*Syd Banks, *Second Chance* (New York: Ballantine, Fawcett Columbine, 1987).

beach with a friend who said to him, "You are not insecure, you just think you are." Syd *heard* that statement so deeply that he could not sleep for three days and three nights because he was experiencing the beauty of life so profoundly for the first time. His *understanding* changed his life as he *saw* the truth about thought in that instant.

This story could give the impression that *understanding* is an all-or-nothing event, which it can be. It can also be a gradual process of levels of understanding. For many of us, understanding deepens as we keep listening from our inner wisdom and inspiration.

Understanding is actually moment-to-moment. We may have *understanding* at one moment, and cover it up with thoughts the next. Or we may have understanding in certain areas and lack understanding in others. In either case, our feelings will let us know. When we experience positivity, we are coming from *understanding;* when we experience negativity, we are coming from a lack of *understanding*. As our understanding deepens, we find more and more joy and serenity in life.

For me, understanding was not instantaneous. When I first heard these principles, my common sense *knew* they were true, but my thought system drove me crazy for a year and a half with "Yes, but," and "How about," and "What if." Even though my old thought system kept getting in the way of my *understanding,* my inner wisdom kept "leading me back" to hear more, and gradually my "Yes, buts; how abouts; and what ifs" changed to "Tell me more."

It is amazing how often we can immediately see the

cause of our negative feelings and laugh at it. At other times thoughts from our thought system may seem so real we would bet our last dollar on them. As our understanding increases, we experience more of the former, and less of the latter.

The learning never ends. Once we get pointed in this direction, life just keeps getting nicer and nicer. Life keeps improving even when there is complete satisfaction with the way things are. George Pransky uses a graphic analogy to explain this phenomenon: It is like waiting at a bus stop for the bus to deeper understanding, but having such a nice time at the bus stop that you don't care if the bus doesn't come. This kind of serenity and satisfaction is found only when we experience life from our natural state of mind.

COMPASS CHART

The following chart is a graphic representation of the conditions we experience when thinking from our natural state of mind, and the conditions we experience when thinking from our programmed thought system.

NATURAL STATE OF MIND	PROGRAMMED THOUGHT SYSTEM
High level of consciousness	*Low level of consciousness*
Security	Insecurity
Love	Judgment
Happiness	Coping
Compassion	Expectations
Satisfaction	Dissatisfaction
Understanding	Assumptions

Insight	Stress
Realization	Rules (shoulds/shouldn'ts)
Forgiveness	Right vs. Wrong
Gratitude	Blame
Sense of humor	Interpretations
Common sense	Anxiety
Wisdom	Proving ego
Inspiration	Inadequacy
Peace of mind	Bitterness
The beauty of now	Past or future oriented
Natural positive feelings	Positive thinking

Try adding other words to the columns. A word such as responsibility feels like duty or compulsiveness when added to the thought system column. Responsibility feels natural and easy when added to the natural state of mind column. Notice how different sex feels in either column, or charity, strength, giving, discipline, teaching, control, or any other concept you can think of. Also notice what happens when you take some of the words from the natural state of mind column and add them to the thought system column; yet how many of us have experienced the contamination of love when we add expectations and judgments? Love and forgiveness, for example, do not have the same feeling when shifted.

We all go in and out of these states of mind every day, depending on what thoughts we are thinking. Remembering that we think makes it natural to change our thoughts, and thus our mental state. Mental illness or mental health is simply a moment-to-moment state of mind. Mental illness and unhappiness are states that occur when we forget that thinking is a function.

Thoughts based on any of the concepts in the column on the right are likely to decrease happiness. Are any of them worth giving up our happiness for?

POSITIVE THINKING— AN ERRONEOUS CONCEPT

Did you wonder why positive thinking was in the column on the right? The control we have over our ability to think is different from the positive thinking commonly taught today, because positive thinkers forget they have the ability to think. They assume that thoughts "happen" to them, and that through positive thinking they can control which thoughts happen or can change the ones that have already happened to them. They are dealing with thinking as a reality rather than as a function.

When we are enjoying a beautiful sunset or feeling love, wouldn't it be ridiculous to stop and say, "I'd better start thinking positive about this." Even to have the thought of positive thinking means we are having negative thoughts, which we think we "should" change. No "shoulds" are involved when we understand the principles, just natural positive feelings and obvious things to do to experience positive results in our lives and relationships. The battleground is eliminated. If we are experiencing a battle in our minds, we are operating from our thought systems, not from our common sense and wisdom.

Positive thinking is also conditional: "I will be happy if I have positive thoughts" or, "I'm a success when I think positive, and a failure when I don't." It is true that we will be happy if we have positive thoughts, but when positive thoughts come from our inner wisdom and inspiration, they are natural and effortless. Have you ever wanted to think positively, but felt like a failure because you couldn't do it? Perhaps what you are learning now will help you understand why it *seems to work* sometimes and not others.

When you see things positively it is not because of positive thinking, but because you *see* positively. Even if you saw something negatively a few moments ago, insight from within, not positive thinking, allows you to *see* it differently.

Annie experienced this after a fight with her brother. She went into her room and tried to forget about it by thinking of enjoyable things. First she thought about baseball, but that didn't work because she just wanted to hit her brother with a baseball bat. Then she tried thinking about soccer, but felt like kicking her brother instead of the ball.

When Annie realized that no kind of thinking helped, she stopped thinking and started looking out the window. She watched the birds and enjoyed looking at the trees and flowers, and soon, instead of thinking positively or negatively about the past, she became engrossed in *now*. Before long, Annie felt good again. She apologized to her brother and spent the rest of the afternoon playing with him.

Positive thinking comes from our programmed thought systems and takes effort. Truly positive thinking is the *natural* expression of beautiful feelings, which come through our natural state of mind in all the positive forms, such as inspiration, gratitude, and unconditional love.

THE BRAIN AS A COMPUTER

The brain is like a perfect computer, but it, too, is only as useful as the software put into it and the operator's ability to run it. Using our distorted thought system is the same as using the old, outdated software—full of bugs. It is also the same as trying to operate a computer without reading the instructions or understanding the basic principles. Both produce unsatisfactory results.

You are now *reading the instructions* and gaining an understanding of the principles that produce beautiful results in life.

Many people do not realize that their thoughts are not them, just as software is not the computer. I have seen several versions of a cartoon showing someone smashing a computer because it wouldn't "work" properly. When we take our negative thoughts seriously, we are using as much sense as that cartoon character, who does not realize the problem is lack of understanding or bugs in the software—not the computer.

Computer buffs know what happens when they try to feed new information into a software program not designed to understand it: the computer beeps and flashes the words "syntax error" on the screen. Even though the new information could improve tremendously the capabilities of the software program, it simply cannot accept the data.

Our brain often does the same thing with new

information that could be very useful to us. When we try to filter this information through our thought system, it "beeps" a lot and says, "wrong!" Fortunately, we have something a computer does not have—inner wisdom and common sense to let us know what new information is useful to improve our lives and relationships, and what information is not useful. We don't have access to the wisdom, however, until we dismiss the thought system.

Dismissing thoughts does not leave a void; it clears the channel so thinking can be used to express common sense, wisdom, and inspiration.

There is a major difference between humans and computers: computers cannot function without software, whereas humans function best without their thought systems.

What thought system (software) are you willing to give up your happiness for?

USING OUR NATURAL STATE OF MIND, RATHER THAN OUR THOUGHT SYSTEM

When we are in higher levels of consciousness, our thoughts will be used to express good feelings. In lower levels of consciousness we use our thought system against ourselves.

Not long ago, I was using my thought system to make myself miserable. Because I thought a friend was being inconsiderate, I was upset; my stomach was churning, and I couldn't sleep. When my feelings let me know what I was doing, I clearly saw that I was giving up my happiness for some negative thoughts. My awareness was followed by a message from my inner wisdom: "Which is worse, being inconsiderate, or being judgmental?" I had to laugh at my self-righteousness. Then I saw that it was not even a matter of being better or worse, because being inconsiderate and judgmental are both simply aspects of thought-provoked insecurity.

Perspective and compassion quickly followed as I remembered the many times I have been inconsiderate—either because I did not know better, or because I believed I was justified. I also realized that just because I thought she was being inconsiderate did not mean she was. All it meant was that she was not living up to some rules and beliefs I had created from my programmed thought system. I laughed at those thoughts also, and could then feel love and gratitude for my friend and for myself.

When happiness is more important to you than anything else, you will be happy, because there will be no thoughts you will be willing to give up your happiness for.

9

Contrary to Popular Opinion

Our programmed thought system is full of many beliefs perpetuated by society that block our inner wisdom, inspiration, and natural good feelings. Therefore, when we have access to our inner wisdom we often see things differently from the mainstream of popular opinion. One of the beliefs perpetuated by popular opinion is that we need rules to live by.

RULES

As our *understanding* deepens, we realize that when living from our natural state of mind we need no rules. Rules are thought-system beliefs that keep us from using our inner wisdom, common sense, and inspiration.

Although much of what I have been teaching may sound like rules, there is a great difference between principles and rules. The examples or generalized suggestions in this book are not meant as rules; their only purpose is to help you get back in touch with your natural good feelings and inner wisdom, often buried under all the rules you have heard and adopted. Some people try to turn the principles into rules, and then wonder why they have negative feelings when they *think* they can't follow them.

Rules are based on thoughts that create insecure feelings, and when feeling insecure, we usually access our thought system rather than our inner wisdom. When our inner wisdom is blocked, we think we need rules, but because they have lost the essence of truth, rules promote more insecure feelings. Deep down our inner wisdom tries to get through and let us know that "this rule does not make sense." We usually ignore this inner guidance, hearing instead our thoughts saying, "You are not following this rule well enough." We then feel inadequate, frustrated, depressed, and more insecure, creating a vicious cycle.

Some people fear that without rules rape, murder, lying, cheating, and stealing would prevail. How silly. Most people would not consider inhumane acts even if there were no laws against them. And people who do are not stopped by laws. Thought-produced insecurity creates negative behavior. People enjoying their natural state of mind do positive things naturally—without rules.

It makes no sense to rely on rules when we have access to our inner wisdom and natural inspiration.

In our natural state of well-being, we will listen to our inner wisdom, and it will not lead us astray. As it guides us through each day, we will experience positive results and enjoy life.

A principle is like a road map: it does not include rules about where we should go, but lets us know where we are, or where we will end up, depending on which direction we go. If we are in Virginia and want to go to New York, it makes no sense to go south. If we are feeling bad, and want to feel good, it makes no sense to use our thought system and take our negative thoughts seriously.

By turning any of the examples or suggestions into rules, we make them a part of our thought system, changing them beyond the recognition of our inner wisdom and common sense so that they are no longer principles.

Rules are like *shoulds,* with a feeling of punishment and reward attached. Principles are natural laws, which simply let us understand the natural consequences of what we do.

When we listen from our heart, we HEAR principles rather than rules.

DOING

What we *do* is a direct result of our *state of mind.* When we allow our natural good feelings to surface (by dismissing negative thoughts), our state of mind is one of love, gratitude, and compassion. In this happy state of mind we have access to inspiration, common sense, and wisdom. What we *do* from a happy state of mind will therefore be different from what we *do* from the state of mind we create through the filters of our thought system.

71

When we are *nice* because we think it is the thing we "should" do, there will be a nagging dissatisfaction. Often there are strings attached—expectations such as, "If I am nice, then things should turn out my way." The world looks and feels different when we get beyond our thought system. When we are *nice* because it feels like the natural thing to do, we will experience satisfaction and contentment. There are no strings attached. There is true joy in the doing.

When I was locked into my thought system, I disliked going to my children's special events, such as soccer and Little League games, but I would go begrudgingly because I thought, "This is what 'good' mothers do."

Because I did not enjoy these events, I would read a book to keep away boredom as well as the *thoughts* of at least twelve other things I *should* be doing.

Recently, however, I spent a full day at three bike races with my son. I did not take a book, and I did not think about twelve other things I should be doing. Instead, I had a good time and showed my interest in the races by asking many questions and by using bike-racing lingo. My son was delighted and said, "You are starting to sound like David's dad." This day at the races was not something I thought I should do; it was what I *felt like* doing as a natural result of feeling content with life and what it has to offer, and I had a wonderful time with my son. Life is so much nicer when viewed from the contentment of one's natural state of mind than from the confusion of the thought system.

Those twelve other things I once *thought* I needed to do were busywork attempts to prove my self-worth, or were used as distractions to escape gnawing discontented feelings. I was on a rat race of *doing;* the twelve things I thought I should do "to prove something" never proved anything, and I would try twelve more. I was missing the enjoyment of my children in favor of the illusion of proving my self-importance, which never brought any lasting satisfaction or contentment. I had turned my back away from lasting treasures to follow the false illusions of silly thoughts.

Sometimes we feel *inspired* to do something nice, but our thoughts sneak in and turn it into a "should." We will know this has happened when our feelings change from ones of happiness to ones of stress and anxiety, or of resentment. A friend shared how this had happened to her. She said she loves baking cookies for friends and family during the holidays, but one year she realized it was no longer fun because she felt she "should" bake cookies for what had become a long list of people. What she had started from her natural state of mind crossed over to her thought system, and the joy was gone.

A FAIRY TALE

Once upon a time there were two fairy princesses, Princess Dew and Princess Bee.

Princess Dew was very busy running around *doing* things for other people—trying to make them happy. Some people loved what Princess Dew did for them, but instead of being happy, they just wanted more. Princess Dew tried hard to do more for them, hoping that someday they would be happy. Other people did not like what she did for them "for their own good," and they wished she would stop interfering.

Princess Dew became worn out, bitter, and frustrated because people did not appreciate all she did for them. She was very unhappy. No one wanted to be around her.

Princess Bee was also very busy—being happy. She enjoyed everything—rainbows and clouds, rainy days and sunny days. She especially enjoyed people. She loved watching them "be." It never occurred to her to interfere in their "being." People loved being around her. Her happiness was contagious.

SERVICE

The fairy tale of Princess Bee and Princess Dew is not meant to imply that we should not do things for others. A happy state of mind will probably inspire us to be of service to others in any way we can. What we do, however, will not come from shoulds or ulterior motives, and it will not be conditional. Service will be for the joy of the moment.

On the other hand, taking care of ourselves is not selfish. The greatest thing we can *do* for ourselves and our relationships is to *BE HAPPY.*

SELFISHNESS

It is popular to have strong negative opinions about selfishness, and, in fact, the selfishness that comes from the thought system looks and feels like the popular descriptions. The selfishness that comes from wisdom and a happy state of mind, however, has a different look and feel.

I know this sounds like double talk until you *see* the difference, which is in the feeling. Selfishness from the thought system is based on ego, self-importance, resentment, rebellion, or total disregard for others; selfishness from a natural, happy state of mind is based on feelings of love and the joy of living. With these feelings, we will want to do whatever our inner wisdom leads us to do to enjoy life.

Because of our old *beliefs* about selfishness, we could let our thought system take over and tell us that what we want to do is "selfish." If we stick to following the feeling from our inner wisdom, we will know the difference—no matter what anyone else thinks.

One day Mary felt like going for a nice, long walk. She received a message from her thought system: "You should not go for a walk when you have so many other things to do, like cleaning the house and shopping." She went for a walk anyway and enjoyed the beautiful day. Her family came home to a happy wife and mother. They enjoyed being around her and felt her love.

Martha also wanted to go for a walk, but she listened to the *shoulds* from her thought system. She felt depressed and did not get much cleaning done. Her family came home to an unhappy wife and mother.

If you are asking, "How will anything ever get done if we always do what we want instead of doing what really needs to be done?" you have missed the point. The next day Martha went for a walk, but still felt depressed. Mary stayed home and cleaned house, and still felt happy.

· From a happy feeling, Mary is able to know what is important for her own well-being and that of her family.

From an unhappy feeling, Martha will feel dissatisfied no matter what she does. For example, Martha has trouble getting her children to do their chores, whereas Mary has inspiration for how to win the cooperation of her children. When Mary cleans house, it is because she enjoys a clean house, not because she is compulsive. When Martha cleans house she is trying to prove that she is a *good* wife and mother.

When we enjoy a nice life, we will be creating serenity in ourselves, in our home, and in the world.

Happiness and peace of mind are contagious.

INTELLIGENCE

Joe commented to Zeke, "I'd rather be smart and miserable than a happy fool."

Wise old Zeke asked, "Is that smart?"

Some people believe that it is a sign of intelligence to find fault and ugliness in the world; they call it *being realistic* and think anyone who can't see the negativity they see is being a blind fool. Of course, these people are not happy when they are being negative.

I prefer a definition of intelligence that includes the wisdom to be happy, no matter what other people think.

Edith Bunker is often a good example. No matter what Archie does, she sees past his behavior and just loves him. Many people criticize Edith, asking, "Doesn't she have enough sense to feel insulted when Archie calls her 'dingbat'?" Actually, Edith has enough of a childlike quality and innocence not to take it personally. Others wonder, "Why doesn't she divorce that chauvinistic pig? She would be much happier without him!" Divorce doesn't even occur to Edith. How could she be happier? Edith is usually happy.

I am not advocating that we all act like Edith Bunker. (After all, she is only the illusion of scriptwriters.) Edith can also be a good example of not seeing things with perspective and common sense; her happiness sometimes depends on others. The point is, once you understand the principles you will see examples of them on television, in literature, and in the way you and others live.

PATIENCE

"I just lost my patience," claimed Helen.

"If only I could be more patient," sighed Henry.

And so the struggle goes when people believe patience is a matter of self-control, or a quality that must be developed. Patience is natural when we experience life through our natural state of mind and feel full of peace and contentment.

Impatience is created from thoughts of dissatisfaction, expectation, or judgment. Dismiss those thoughts and you have patience, because it is impossible to feel impatient and satisfied at the same time.

You may ask, "How can I possibly be patient when someone is doing something I know they should not be doing?" Turning the other cheek always seemed terribly wimpy to me. It makes sense now. When we *see* the innocence in what others do from a lack of understanding, it makes no sense to lash out at them, or to lose our own peace of mind in reaction to their insecurity. It does make sense to create a loving, forgiving atmosphere in which they can best gain understanding, or to know when they are not ready to learn.

FORGIVENESS

An unwillingness to forgive is one of the greatest blocks to our natural state of mind and is based on ego, expectations, judgments, lack of compassion, and a belief that there is only one possible reality—mine! There is only one thing to be gained by not forgiving—misery!

People who have the popular opinion that forgiveness is something you have to *work at* or *try to do,* are engrossed in ego and judgment. It is a superiority trip to think, "Well, I know you did something 'wrong,' but I will be 'big' enough to *forgive* you." Or, "You did a despicable thing, and you don't deserve forgiveness." Lack of forgiveness comes from self-righteous judgment and harms the unforgiving more than the unforgiven. *It is impossible to be happy while holding onto (rather than dismissing) judgments.*

Anyone who says, "I will forgive, but I won't forget," does not *understand* forgiveness: forgiveness *is* forgetting. It is realizing that ego, expectations, and judgments are thoughts that are just not worth hanging on to, and, when we let go of them, they are forgotten. Dismissing negative thoughts and forgiving are synonymous.

Forgiveness is natural from a level of consciousness that includes understanding, compassion, love, humor, gratitude, and peace of mind. Forgiveness is not even an issue when we have these feelings, because when we *see* with *understanding* there is nothing to forgive.

CIRCUMSTANCES

Contrary to popular opinion, circumstances have nothing to do with happiness.

We often hear, "I'll be happy when I finish school. I'll be happy when I'm married. I'll be happy when I'm single. I'll be happy when I have more money. I'll be happy when I have children. I'll be happy when I don't have children. I'll be happy when *you* do what I want you to do."

If you are not happy before you get what you want, you won't be happy after you get it. Happiness is a state of mind.

If you are not happy before you get married, you won't be happy after you get married. If you are not happy before you have children, you won't be happy after you have children. If you are not happy with your children, you won't be happy after they are gone. If you are not happy married, you won't be happy single—at least not for long. People who think they are happy when they first get what they want find it doesn't last long. When things settle down they feel that old, nagging insecurity and dissatisfaction, or they get trapped back in their feelings of unhappiness the first time things don't go the way they *think* they should.

One man questioned this principle. He asked, "Do you mean to tell me that losing my legs would not be a reason for me to be unhappy?"

He was told, "That is right. It is only what you could think about losing your legs that could create unhappiness."

He said, "That is the most stupid thing I ever heard of."

Another man who was listening spoke up, "It is true. I lost both my legs in Vietnam, but I have never been happier. That does not mean I don't wish I had my legs. I would love to have my legs back, but I didn't know how to be happy when I had them. Now I know how to be happy even without them."

Happiness is a state of mind that allows us to *see* things differently. In a happy state of mind (our natural state of mind) we *see* life with gratitude and perspective, and circumstances look different from how they appear when seen through the filter of our thought system. When we are in a happy state of mind, what *to do* comes from inspiration; what to do seems obvious, and will be loving. There are no strings attached, because we realize our happiness has nothing to do with external circumstances.

Happiness is a state of mind that comes from WITHIN.

You may be wondering, "But what about things that are beyond my control, like sickness or negative things other people do?" When we have peace of mind and contentment we see *what is* without judgment like the wise man in the following story.

A HORSE STORY

Many years ago a wise man lived in an old mountain village. One day a beautiful, wild stallion ran into his corral. When the villagers heard the news they came to his farm and marveled, "What a wonderful thing! You are so lucky!"

The wise man replied, "Maybe so, maybe not."

A few days later the stallion broke the corral fence and ran away. When the villagers heard the news they came to his farm and said, "What a terrible thing! What bad luck!"

The wise man replied, "Maybe so, maybe not."

The next day the stallion returned, bringing a whole herd of mares. When the villagers heard the news they came and exclaimed, "Now you are the richest man in the village, and surely the luckiest!"

The wise man replied, "Maybe so, maybe not."

The wise man's son tried to break one of the mares, but was thrown and broke his leg. When the villagers heard the news they came and sympathized, "What a tragedy! Who will help you now with the harvest? This is such an unlucky thing to happen!"

The wise man replied, "Maybe so, maybe not."

The next day the Cossacks came to get all the young men of the village to fight in their wars. They did not take the wise man's son because of his broken leg.

SEEING WHAT IS WITHOUT JUDGMENT

You may ask, "But what if I'm not in a state of mind that allows me to *see* things without judgment? What if I do have negative thoughts and feelings about external circumstances?"

The most helpful thing is to accept, and have compassion for, yourself as you are—without judgment.

When we are confronted with circumstances we can't seem to *understand* and we add negative thoughts to them, we have two things we dislike—the circumstances and our negative thoughts about them. Our thoughts are usually much worse than the circumstances. It is our thoughts that produce our feelings.

We don't *see* the beauty of life or experience feelings of joy and gratitude when we waste time and energy on judgments. Judgments fill us with toxic feelings.

A good example is the story of two men who lost their fortunes. One had negative thoughts about his circumstances and jumped off a building. The other man *saw* them as an opportunity to have the adventure of starting over again in something new.

By the way, the man who jumped off the building was not a happy person even when he had his fortune, whereas the man who *saw* the opportunity had been enjoying life during all of his varied circumstances.

WHO, ME? I THOUGHT IT WAS YOU, IT, THEM!

Your world is created by how you *see* it, and how you *see* it is directly related to the filters in your thought system, or to your lack of filters. An absence of filters allows you to *see* the world freshly from your natural state of mind.

Do I hear an argument? "I can understand how that applies to most circumstances, but not to others." People often try to find extreme cases where they think a principle "might" not be true, in order to invalidate it, instead of simply applying the principle to situations in their own lives, where they *know* it is true.

I have found that as I experience the principles in

areas where I do not doubt, my understanding deepens. I then doubt less and *see* the principles in areas I have formerly been unable to understand. This is a progression that never ends. *Understanding* keeps deepening, and life keeps getting more beautiful. Actually, life is always beautiful. We either *see* it or we don't.

10

Detours

There are many detours that keep us from the treasures
of happiness and peace of mind.

INSECURITY

Insecurity is just another thought. There is really no
such thing. *Try to feel insecure without thinking you are
insecure.* It is impossible!

Many therapists try to help others, even while
believing in their own insecurities. They claim, "At least I
know how to cope with my insecurities. I know how to
handle them." These therapists are not much better off
than their clients, because they still see insecurity as
reality rather than as a thought. Coping may be better
than not coping, but it falls far short of happiness and
peace of mind. Even though insecurity is just another
thought, it becomes very powerful when taken seriously.

Thought-provoked insecurity may take many
forms, such as aggressiveness, drug abuse, shyness, the

need to prove one's worth through power or achieve-
ments, wars, self-righteousness, or feelings of inadequacy. Every negative act is based on thoughts that
produce the illusion of insecurity, followed by each
individual's interpretations of what he or she needs to
do to overcome or hide from the illusionary insecurity.

Like other illusions, insecurity loses its power once
we know what it is. *Understanding* inspires love and
compassion for ourselves, as well as for others who may
not know their negative behavior is based on the illusion
of insecurity.

JUDGMENTS

One form of judgment is very helpful. For example, if
we see a truck speeding toward us, we will probably
make the judgment that it would be a good idea to get
out of the way. To add the *judgment* that every truck is
dangerous, and stuff our thought systems with a fear of
trucks, would be a useless burden.

Many excuse their judgment of others by calling it
righteous judgment. Righteous judgment is rare;
because it is based on feelings of love and understanding, it leaves no negative feelings in its wake. Instead, the
results of righteous judgment are positive.

"I'm telling you this for your own good," is not an
example of righteous judgment, but of taking your own
separate reality seriously and thinking it is the "right"
reality. Self-righteous judgment of others is not helpful;
it leaves negative feelings. Negative feelings are the compass that lets us know we are caught up in our thought
system. As soon as we become aware of our thought

system, it loses power. When we dismiss judgment for the thought that it is, we rise to a higher level of consciousness where judgments are replaced with love, compassion, and inspiration about what to do.

Debra was having negative feelings about her friend Georgia, who was living her life in ways that "looked" negative to Debra. Debra decided to stay away from her for awhile, which could have been a reasonable solution if Debra had kept it simple and stayed away without judgment of Georgia or herself. Debra contaminated her decision, however, by judging herself. "If I were a bigger person, I wouldn't let her behavior bother me. I should be more loving and understanding." Her thoughts of self-judgment kept her in a low mood, limiting her perspective and producing more judgments of her friend. "She is being so self-centered, self-righteous, manipulative, and self-serving. She thinks her reality is the only valid one in the world." Debra was able to find several others who had the same judgments about Georgia, which she saw as justification for her thoughts.

Debra's stomach was in knots as she continued the vicious cycle of self-condemnation and judgment of Georgia. Finally she saw her judgments for the thoughts they were and, as soon as she dismissed them, was able to stay away from a situation that did not feel good to her, without judgment of herself or her friend. She realized that someday her understanding might deepen enough that her friend's behavior would not bother her, but until then she would stay away, without judgment. She even saw that she could possibly be wrong or lacking in understanding of the whole picture, but simply was not now able to see with perspective.

There is a world of difference between walking away from a situation with judgment, and walking away without judgment. Our common sense may tell us to walk away from a situation, but it will not tell us to judge it, in the sense of having negative feelings against someone or something.

Being without judgment is being in a *state of humility and quiet.* During the "quiet," Debra's *understanding* deepened. The next time she saw Georgia, her negative feelings were gone. In her new state of understanding, she had a deeper appreciation of everything in life, including her friend Georgia. She knew that what she had seen in Georgia before was only a reflection of thoughts and *beliefs* about how things "should be" according to the reality of her ego.

STEREOTYPING

Another danger of judgment is that we often judge a person for what they do when they are in a *bad mood,* and decide this is the sum total of *who they are.* Often we dismiss what they do when they are in a good mood as "just an act." In so doing, we have taken the detour of believing in the reality of one mood and refusing to see other possibilities. We are more willing to trust the validity of behavior from a low mood than behavior from a high mood.

JUDGMENTS FROM OTHERS

With *understanding,* we pay no more attention to the judgments of others than to our own. We see that we get into enough trouble taking our own judgments seriously, and that *shoulds* and *shouldn'ts* are no more helpful from others than they are from ourselves. This does not mean we will judge other people's thoughts; we will simply know that they are just thoughts, and then we will see them with compassion, interest, or humor.

Virginia dreaded being around her mother for long because she felt intimidated by her judgments, which she reacted to with rebellion. Her mother reacted to Virginia's rebellion with more judgments.

After learning about the principles, Virginia spent a delightful four days traveling across the country with her mother. As Virginia tells the story, "Every time my mom came out with what I used to call a judgment, I just saw it as her reality. Instead of rebelling and letting her know that I thought what she thought was stupid, I saw it as interesting. I still didn't agree with her on everything, but I respected her right to see things differently. I was also able to respect my own way of seeing things, without getting huffy about it. We had a great time. We talked and shared more than we have in my whole life."

LIVING FOR OR AGAINST SOMEONE ELSE

Often we take the detour of trying to live up to the expectations of others and become "approval junkies" and "pleasers." By doing so, we discount our own inner wisdom and inspiration. Other times we take the detour of rebelling against the expectations of others, even when following their suggestions might be to our benefit.

Once there was a little girl named Marie who went to visit her aunt and uncle and learned how to make bread. Her aunt and uncle thought that was wonderful and praised her and told her over and over how much they appreciated her bread.

Marie went home and baked bread for her family. No one said anything about her bread, but just ate it. Marie decided she would never make bread for her family again because they didn't appreciate it and praise her.

Then one day she discovered she enjoyed making bread for the fun of it. She loved getting her hands into the dough to knead it; she loved the aroma of the baking bread; and she especially loved eating it hot out of the oven, dripping with butter and sometimes honey. She also loved sharing it with anyone who wanted to have some. She realized that when she was living "for" or "against" someone else, she missed the bread.

EGO AND SELF-IMPORTANCE

The illusion of insecurity is strongly connected with the illusions of ego and proving self-importance. Ego assumes there is something to prove, and the need to prove self-importance is based on the assumption that it is possible not to be important. In a sense this is true, because being important usually means *more important than someone else,* which we are not. But we are important, just because we exist.

It is impossible to find happiness through trying to prove self-importance. The basis for the search (the belief that it is possible to be unimportant) guarantees failure. Temporary relief might be found through some kind of achievement, but it doesn't last. These people keep believing they are insecure, while trying to prove their insecurity doesn't exist. It is exhausting even to think about it. When you get off track into your thought system, notice how often the detour is related to issues challenging your thoughts and beliefs about proving your self-importance or challenging how you think life or others should be. It is strenuous just to think about all the silly antics we go through in life to try to prove something that has no need to be proven.

We forget that we created our ego, and we let it take control.

We create our ego to protect our thought system. Isn't that ironic? We create something to protect something that should not be protected, but should be recognized for what it is and not taken seriously. We give up who we really are (in our natural state of mind) when we program our thought system. We live our lives through a faulty program that produces misery, and then create an ego to ensure the faulty program's survival.

I used to scoff at the question, "Who am I?" Now it makes sense because I realize I am different when experiencing life through my natural state of mind from when experiencing life through my thought system and ego.

The fun thing about ego is that every time we recognize it for what it is, we can't help laughing at it, thus making it disappear. Our ego loves catching us off guard, however, so that it can sneak back. You can now play hide-and-seek with your ego.

We can have perspective when observing ego in

others, but often lose that perspective when it comes to ourselves. We have fun pointing out others' false egos (unless we turn judgmental), and life will be nicer when we can have as much fun catching our own egos.

Being concerned about the judgments of others is just another ego trip. When we are ego-involved, we can feel intimidated about what others say. When we dismiss ego, we are not affected by what others say. We may choose to consider feedback, but won't be intimidated.

SELF-CENTERING ON SELF-ESTEEM

Self-esteem is the natural well-being you feel when you stop centering on your *ego*. Self-esteem is like happiness: you can't find it by looking for it. We have inherent and natural self-esteem and happiness when we dismiss the thought system that keeps them buried.

An extremely popular detour is the one of "working on" self-esteem. Since lack of self-esteem is an illusion that exists only with thoughts from the thought system, it makes no sense to give the illusion credibility by trying to attain self-esteem. The idea that a person could not have self-worth is a very silly thought and is based on other silly thoughts about what a person must "do, be, achieve, look like, or own." It is much easier simply to dismiss thoughts that create the illusion of lack of self-esteem.

Being *self*-centered on *self*-esteem is a detour guaranteed to lead you away from your natural self-esteem.

ANGER

It takes little to make me angry when my ego thoughts are in control. I get angry when people don't drive the way I want them to and when my husband doesn't respond the way I want him to, at exactly the moment I want him to (preferably by reading my mind). I get angry when my family and friends don't behave the way I want them to or don't always live up to my expectations. I get angry when equipment doesn't work the way I want it to and when business people don't think I am the most important customer they have. I especially get angry when someone else gets angry at me. This is about one-tenth of my list.

We get angry when our thoughts that create ego and self-importance decide the world should revolve around us. We can spend a lot of time on this detour away from happiness, since the world never does revolve around us.

When I see my anger as reality, I have different ways of expressing it. Sometimes I verbalize anger, sometimes I sulk, and sometimes I have a silent tantrum against myself and get depressed.

My list of justifications as to why the world should revolve around me is much shorter. It *should* because my reality is the "right" one. Thoughts that create ego and thoughts that create self-righteousness walk through our thought system hand-in-hand.

Anger is nothing more than ego being expressed in a tantrum. I jokingly and fondly refer to this as SBS (spoiled brat syndrome). I once was president of the SBS

Club, but the club was abolished when I learned that anger and SBS exist only with thought.

There is a popular opinion that if you don't get your anger out, you will store it, and it will fester. This is not true. Anger festers when you keep taking negative thoughts seriously and keep thinking about them. When you forget about the thoughts that create negative feelings, they are not stored. You have to think about the thoughts again to re-create the bad feelings. If you think about those negative thoughts again, after forgetting about them for awhile, it is not because they were stored. You were simply distracted from thinking about them, even though you still took them seriously, and then re-created them.

Another popular belief is that there are certain things that justify anger. Not true again. Anger does not solve anything; it just makes you feel bad and keeps you from enjoying life *NOW,* or from accessing your inner wisdom to know what to do.

Christine Heath, now a therapist at the Hawaii Mental Health Institute, worked in group-therapy sessions with sixty women, victims of rape or incest. For many years these women talked about their anger, beat on pillows, and yelled and screamed about their anger. They spent hours confirming that what had happened to them in the past was the reason they could not hold jobs, were alcoholics, and could not participate in lasting relationships.

After Christine learned about the principles, she apologized to the women in her groups, "I'm sorry, ladies, but I have been doing it all wrong. From now on we will no longer dwell on the past, but will talk about some principles that will teach you how to have happiness and peace of mind in life now."

A few women dropped out because they did not want to give up their anger. The remaining women soon learned to enjoy life. A two-year follow-up showed they maintained their good feelings and were successful in their jobs and relationships. Some were training to become therapists or educators so they could share what they had learned.

One woman who had been raped appeared on a panel with other rape victims. She was obviously a very happy person. The moderator of the panel questioned her, "Don't you feel angry? Hasn't your rape experience affected your relationship with men? Why are you so happy?"

She answered, "That experience took up eleven minutes of my life. I don't intend to give it one more second. Life is so full of good things to enjoy, why should I waste time thinking about the past?"

When we don't like what happened in the past, it doesn't make sense to keep re-creating it in our thoughts, and then to multiply the unhappiness we create by adding anger. Like all negative thoughts, anger loses its power when seen with perspective. As soon as you can laugh at anger, or at least see it for what it is, anger is gone.

THE PAST

Another popular detour is into the past. The past cannot exist unless we think about it, yet many live their whole lives on this detour.

Our brain does not store what happened in the past. Instead, the thought system stores our interpretations of what happened, and these interpretations (thoughts) create our emotions. Because it is impossible to store emotions, we keep re-creating the same negative emotions when we keep thinking about our old interpretations. Our interpretations are hardly ever correct; any time we choose to interpret an event differently, our emotions and reactions will also change.

Linda had an experience in her past in which it seemed to her that her father had felt embarrassed to hug her. She interpreted that to mean he didn't love her, which she interpreted to mean she was not lovable. If she was not lovable to her own father, that must mean she was not lovable to anyone. So she started living her life feeling insecure because of her thought that she was unlovable. She constantly tried to prove she was lovable, but because her behavior was based on insecurity, she acted demanding and unlovable. Besides, as she really believed she was not lovable, she would not have accepted any evidence that she was lovable. She would constantly ask her husband if he really loved her. He was very patient and kept reassuring her that he did. Linda either wouldn't believe him or would lose respect for him for loving such an unlovable person. This all became hilarious to her once she dismissed her interpretations and thoughts of insecurity and saw the ridiculousness of the whole comedy.

When stuck in any of these illusions of the past, we miss life. Yet many people believe these illusions are real—that they are life. All this insanity is eliminated through *understanding* thought.

When we understand that the past exists only when we think about it and is only our interpretation of what happened, it becomes difficult to take our thoughts about the past seriously. In the same way, when we see the innocence of others' past actions, knowing they did the best they could from their then-level of understanding, we will feel differently about those actions.

Another woman who had been raped spent years hating and distrusting all men. When she realized what she was doing, she changed her perspective totally and went into prisons to work with rapists. She was able to change many lives when she worked from love and compassion.

Paula often complained about all the terrible things her mother had done and said to her in the past. A therapist asked her, "Do you think your mother stayed up late at night plotting ways to make your life miserable?"

With reluctance, Paula admitted, "No."

A week later Paula shared that she had gained much insight from that question. It had become clear to her that her mother really did love her, and had done the best she could based on her own insecurities.

Paula added that she was now able to *see* how she was repeating many of the same "mistakes" with her own son and gave the following example: "I punish him when he makes mistakes, even though I hated it when my mother did that. I can see now that she probably did it for the same reasons I do. I'm afraid that if I don't punish him he won't learn to do better, and I want him to do better because I love him. But when I was a child I can remember wishing my mother would understand how I felt and teach me with love instead of punishment."

Paula was able to forgive her mother and herself when she *understood* that the "mistakes" they had both made were simply the results of getting sidetracked from love and enjoyment of their children into thoughts that produced fear and insecurity.

DECISIONS

Contrary to common behavior, it is not helpful to *figure things out* or make decisions when feeling stress. This only keeps us deeply enmeshed in our thought system. It is as ineffective as keeping our foot on the gas pedal to get out of a ditch, while the spinning wheel digs deeper and deeper into the sand.

If you have any doubts about what to do, or want to do something because of negative feelings such as anger, let that be your clue that you are *lost in your thought system.* Get quiet and wait for your negative feelings to pass so your natural state of mind can surface.

Decisions from our natural state of mind are always positive and produce good results. We know when decisions are inspiration from our inner wisdom and need not doubt their appropriateness.

Actually, the concept of decision changes with *understanding.* The familiar concept of decision implies choice or effort. With *understanding,* decisions feel more like obvious, common-sense things to do than like choice or effort.

A decision may make sense in one situation. If we

make a rule out of it, however, we will lose touch with our inner wisdom and inspiration. No matter how similar the situation is, it may call for a completely different decision at another time. Only our common sense knows.

One day I realized I had made a rule out of not spreading my low moods around. In other words, I had decided I *should* never talk about it. Now I can see that not talking about it is a decision that makes sense some of the time. One day I felt like talking with a good friend about a situation I knew I was seeing through my judgmental glasses. My *shoulds* got very busy in my thought system. "I *should* not be spreading this around. I *should* be able to dismiss it and go to a higher level of consciousness." Then my ego joined in, "He is going to think I don't know anything since I can't stay at a high level of consciousness." I talked about it anyway, and while I was listening to myself and to him, I gained insights that made it easy and natural to dismiss my judgments and *see* with perspective again.

I was again reminded that the principles are not a basis for judgment regarding *shoulds* or *shouldn'ts,* but are the means to give us an understanding of what happens when we do what we do.

LIGHTEN UP, KEEP IT SIMPLE, AND COME FROM LOVE

When I am miserably on my way down the path of low moods I have usually taken three detours at once. I have taken my perceptions seriously (usually having to do with ego, expectations, and judgments of myself or others). I have then tried to analyze complicated ways to solve the problem—all of which make jumping off a bridge seem like the best solution. And third, I am coming from perceptions of insecurity that manifest themselves in anger, hatred, and hopelessness. In other words, from this state of mind all the possible, complicated solutions don't really seem like solutions at all, but more like ways of seeking revenge or escape. What a detour!

As soon as I tune into my inner wisdom (sometimes in minutes, sometimes in days) I can see what I have done and feel inspired to lighten up, keep it simple, and come from love.

Lightening up usually means simply raising your perspective so you see the big picture. When you lighten up and quit taking things seriously, what once seemed like a tragedy can now be seen as an interesting event—a stepping-stone rather than a stumbling block—as a great gift full of lessons to be learned, or as just a humorous situation.

Keeping it simple usually means that the solution becomes obvious and uncomplicated when you drop the anger, hatred, and revenge. Trying to figure things out from our thought system is usually complicated; figuring things out from our natural state of mind is simple.

Coming from love means that what you do is not as important as how you do it. For example, maybe it would be a wise thing to ground your child or fire an employee or leave a relationship. This can be done with love and respect rather than with anger and revenge.

When you are doing the obvious thing to handle a situation, there is no need for anger. Lighten up, keep it simple, and come from love.

IT GETS EASIER TO AVOID DETOURS

Even a limited understanding of the principles keeps us pointed in the right direction so that our understanding keeps getting deeper. The deeper the understanding, the easier it gets.

Let good feelings from your common sense and wisdom be your only guide.

11

Relationships

The principles show us where all problems in a relationship originate:

1. Trying to change realities—fighting over who is right instead of respecting differences and finding them interesting.

2. Getting caught up in negative thoughts—judgments, interpretations, the past, proving ego and self-importance, spoiled bratness, and other forms of thought-produced insecurity—which happens when we focus on the content of our thoughts instead of realizing thinking is a function.

3. Not dismissing negative thoughts during low moods or low levels of consciousness, but instead, trying to discuss them, figure them out, or solve them.

4. Sharing negative feelings that come from the insecurity of our thought systems, with the belief that our partners should understand them, take them seriously, and adopt them as their own reality, instead of waiting for the negative feelings to pass and sharing the positive feelings that come from our natural state of mind.

SEPARATE REALITIES
RELATING TO RELATIONSHIPS

Amy and Sean had daily arguments. No matter what the subject, the theme was always the same.

Amy: "You have to be blind as a bat not to see things my way!"

Sean: "If you had any brains at all, you would know that my way is right!"

What good are eyes and brains without understanding and wisdom? Amy and Sean are both stuck in the illusions of their separate realities.

Have you ever tried to convince your partner that your point of view was the right one, and felt as if you were talking to a wall? You were actually talking to two walls—the wall of your own unique reality and the wall of your partner's unique reality. Literally talking to a wall could be easier because a wall does not have its own point of view. You wouldn't have any expectations from a wall; in fact you would feel pretty silly trying to convince a wall that your interpretation of *how things are* is the "right" interpretation.

It is even less productive to try convincing your partner, who already *knows* how things *are* and would like to convince you. Your partner is usually seeing his or her reality with as much perspective as you are seeing yours: zero.

Jeannette strongly believed her children needed lots of rules and guidance; Duane believed he should sacrifice anything important to him in order to cater to their whims. Duane thought Jeannette was a tyrant; Jeannette thought Duane was a wimp. Both were so lost in their separate realities and thought systems that they could not *see* clearly or with perspective. All the children needed were love and wisdom. Sometimes wisdom might take the form of guidance, sometimes the form of doing things with or for them. In either case, guidance or doing things for them based on good feelings and inspiration will be different from those actions based on self-righteousness, defensiveness, or judgment.

When we take our reality seriously, it becomes an interesting frame of reference—or a distorted pair of glasses. We don't realize how those glasses distort and filter everything in our world. When we dismiss our judgments and expectations, we *see* a very different and interesting person in front of us.

Dorene and Charles were experiencing marital difficulty because they were deeply enmeshed in their separate realities. Their distorted frames of reference prevented them from seeing anything with common sense and wisdom.

Dorene complained about being third or fourth priority in Charles's life. This thought quickly became a belief from which she was able to generate hurt feelings. She continued to complicate matters by thinking she needed to cover her hurt feelings with anger, by which she gained a false sense of security. She expressed her anger by blaming and attacking Charles for not putting her first.

Charles took her attacks seriously and generated feelings of inadequacy and defensiveness which he expressed by acting disdainful toward Dorene. Charles's frame of reference included a belief that women were unfair and unreasonable anyway.

Dorene and Charles were unaware that they were not seeing the circumstances and each other clearly in the present, but through distorted past beliefs programmed into their thought systems.

Somewhere in Dorene's past she had had an experience she had interpreted to mean that she was unimportant. She turned this interpretation into a belief that distorted every experience she had from then on. Without being aware of what she was doing, she spent her life looking for evidence to support her belief in her unimportance, and she was so intent on this task that she missed any evidence that might change her belief.

This was obvious when she told the story of how she and Charles met and got married. Charles was dating Adele, but quit seeing her and soon asked Dorene to marry him. Dorene did not see this as evidence that she was important to Charles. What she did notice was Adele's name on the wedding invitation list, which she saw as evidence that Adele was more important to him than she was. Explanations from Charles that he still liked Adele as a friend fell on deaf ears.

Charles had had an experience in his past that he had interpreted to mean that women were unfair and unreasonable. He adopted this as such a strong belief that he was unaware of how he *set women up* to prove he was right. In this case, he knew Dorene would probably be upset if he put Adele's name on the list, but, although it wasn't important to have Adele come to the wedding, he wanted to be able to prove he was right about how unreasonable women can be. Of course, he claimed it was important because he had to justify his position.

You and I have enough perspective (because we are removed) to see the humor in their silly thinking, but Dorene and Charles were not laughing. When we take the filters from our thought system seriously, it is impossible to see the situation with perspective.

Dorene and Charles were focused on what they were looking for through the filters of their thought systems, which left little time to share good feelings. When our attention is focused on looking for evidence to support our distorted beliefs, we miss the obvious, wonderful things going on around us. For example, suppose I told you that I had hidden a red button in a beautifully decorated room and would give you $10,000 if you could find it in five minutes. You would probably find it. Then suppose I said, "Fine. I'll give you the $10,000; but I'll give you $20,000 if you can describe the room to me." Do you think you could describe the room? Of course not. You would have missed everything around you because you were focused on looking for the red button.

We can always create what we are looking for. For instance, if we believe we will be rejected, we will act in such a way that invites rejection, or we will see rejection even in innocent behaviors that do not mean rejection at all.

It is impossible, however, for anyone to reject another person. If someone says you are the biggest creep in the world, that statement actually has nothing to do with you. People who make remarks such as this are simply caught up in their own thought systems and are feeling insecure.

Dorene and Charles finally dismissed their insecurities and saw each other very differently. They stopped playing detectives looking for evidence to support their insecurities. Charles felt like reassuring Dorene that she was important, and Dorene felt like reassuring Charles that she trusted him. Neither one really needed reassurance any more, but each accepted the loving gestures. They had learned to laugh at their silly thoughts and *see* the beauty of life and of each other.

ACCEPTANCE

Acceptance means respecting differences, not conditional acceptance while waiting for changes to be made or tolerance for someone who obviously has not learned the "right way." Acceptance is seeing that everyone has a separate reality. From our natural state of mind, we will *see* levels of insecurity in others with compassion. From our thought system, we will see behavior through our filters of judgment.

Even though it is impossible to change other people's realities (only they can do that by changing their own thoughts), we often keep trying.

A marriage counselor suggested to Hazel that she stop trying to change her husband and accept him the way he was. Three months later Hazel complained, "But I have accepted him for three whole months, and he hasn't changed a bit!" What Hazel thought was acceptance was conditional. True acceptance is unconditional and allows us to *see* a different reality—a reality full of gratitude, peace of mind, and joy, as illustrated in the following poem.

Acceptance

When I want
  more of you
I'm truly in love
  with you.

When I want you
  to be more
I'm in love
  with a dream.

Wanting you to be more
  makes me (and you) miserable.
Wanting more of you
  fulfills my dreams.

When I want more
  of you
I *see* you
  in all your
    specialness
    uniqueness
    magnificence
and

       I am filled
   with gratitude
   wonder
   joy.

You mean so much to me.

I want more of you.

THOUGHTS AND MOODS
RELATED TO RELATIONSHIPS

Mary thought Jim was not paying enough attention to her. When she self-righteously shared this with her friends, they told her the importance of letting him know how she felt. Mary decided that was a good idea, so that night when Jim sat down on the couch and started to read the newspaper, she sat next to him and said, "How come the newspaper is more important to you than I am?"

Jim defensively retorted, "Because the newspaper doesn't hassle me."

Mary ran to the bedroom and cried, and for the rest of the evening she did not speak to Jim. The next day she told all her friends that Jim had admitted he preferred the newspaper to her, so she might as well get a divorce.

Fortunately Mary had an opportunity to learn about the principles. She dismissed the notions of insecurity from her thought system and was amazed how much her feelings about herself and Jim changed when she saw the world from her natural state of mind.

The next time Jim sat down to read the newspaper, she sat quietly next to him, feeling gratitude for having such a nice man for a husband. She could see past his insecure behavior and felt unconditional love because she had dismissed her own insecurities, judgments, and expectations.

Soon Jim put down the newspaper and gruffly asked, "Did you want to talk?"

Mary could feel that he was still in a bad mood and replied, "No, I was just enjoying your presence." Suspiciously, Jim continued to read the newspaper. For several weeks Mary continued to enjoy just being with Jim, no matter what he did. She had discovered her own inner happiness and peace of mind and was not affected by outside circumstances.

One day Jim came into the kitchen while Mary was preparing dinner. She asked, "Did you want something?"

"No," Jim replied, "I just wanted to be with you."

Some people who hear this story think Mary acted like a wimp who decided to passively put up with a jerk. Look at her results: she found serenity, saw the goodness beneath Jim's insecurity-based actions, and inspired him to experience his own natural state of mind. Another person might follow his or her wisdom to do something else. When living in a natural state of mind there are infinite possibilities about what to do, but the feelings behind the doing will be the same—compassion, serenity, respect, forgiveness, gratitude, and all the other feelings that are the essence of love.

We create our world from our thoughts and actions. *We reap what we sow:* when we put negativity out into the world, we get negativity back. Yet when negativity comes back, most people forget they put it out in the first place; they don't take responsibility for its creation by their thoughts and subsequent actions. In the same way, when we put positivity out into the world, positivity comes back.

You know you are feeling positive when you feel so grateful for *what is* that you don't expect anything back. Expecting something back is manipulative, conditional giving.

Are you still arguing that sometimes negative circumstances come to you even when you did nothing to create them? Even if you have no personal responsibility for the creation of certain events, your thoughts give you more trouble than the circumstances do.

Sue's husband had an affair, and she was so hurt by this that she wanted revenge. She went to an attorney and said, "I want to hurt him as much as he hurt me. I want to leave him with as little as possible financially, and to limit his child visitation rights as much as possible. I will make sure the kids don't even want to see him."

Sue could not *see* that it was her thoughts about this situation that were making her miserable. Fortunately she chose a wise attorney, who asked, "Do you really want to hurt him in the worst way possible?"

Sue replied, "Yes."

The attorney said, "Then go back and live with him for six months. Be the very best wife you can imagine: be loving, compassionate, understanding, forgiving, affectionate, and fun to be with. He will feel lucky and will start loving you very much. In six months you can start divorce proceedings, which will hurt him emotionally and financially."

Sue objected, "I couldn't stand to live with him for six more months."

The attorney said, "Well, then you must not really want to hurt him in the worst way possible."

Sue said, "Oh yes I do. I will do it."

Two years later the attorney saw Sue walking down a street. He asked, "What happened? I thought you were going to come back for a divorce."

Sue replied, "Are you kidding? He is the most wonderful man in the world. I wouldn't even think of leaving him." Sue must have done such a good job acting loving that she soon forgot it was an act and started enjoying the good feelings. Good feelings are extremely contagious, creating more good feelings in most people who come in contact with them, as happened with Sue and her husband.

When *understanding* changes how we *see* things, everything and everyone in our world looks different. It may seem as though others have changed, but it is our thoughts, and thus our reality, and thus our feelings that have changed. Others often respond to our feeling level. When we give love, we get love—not necessarily because others give it back to us, but because love will emanate from within. Feeling love does not depend on anything or anyone else.

You may ask, "But, what if I just don't feel loving, and I am not willing to 'act' as Sue did?" Whenever we feel the need to ask what to do, it is helpful to do nothing except dismiss our thoughts, get quiet, and wait until we feel good enough to know from our own wisdom what to do.

And if you don't feel ready, you don't feel ready.

What is, is. To simply accept what is can be very calming.

Remember that sometimes awareness of the principles will change our mood instantly, and we will tap into our natural state of mind and inner wisdom. Other times we may see that focusing on the content of our thoughts is producing our negative feelings, but we won't feel totally better immediately. Those times are more like when we have the flu; we have a level of understanding that doesn't change our state of mind immediately, but it may lead us to quietly take care of ourselves until our mood passes.

I realized this after an experience of being *caught up* in thinking my reality was much better than my husband's. I really believed he was wrong, and since it seemed so real to me, I certainly had to tell him about it. Have you ever noticed that when you think other people are "wrong," you feel compelled to inform them? Have you also noticed that you become *worse,* with your judgments, criticisms, and self-righteousness, than the person you are judging? (*Worse* is just another judgment not to be taken seriously. Look for the principle.)

My tirade lasted about five minutes before my miserable feelings alerted me to *see* what I was doing. Although I immediately shut up, I still didn't feel much better; I simply *saw* enough to get quiet and quit spreading my negative emotions around. I started thinking, "I should apologize." But I didn't feel like apologizing, since I was still in a relatively low state of mind, so I just stayed quiet.

I forget how long it took me to feel better, because I stopped thinking about my negative emotions, but the next day when I was feeling love and gratitude for my husband, we talked about what had happened. Since I was then in a loving mood, it felt natural to apologize without feeling blame and guilt. Barry shared that he was aware my silence the day before was different from my old sulky silences that sent out vibrations of anger and blame. He said, "It was very nice."

Another time I became upset when my husband and I missed an opportunity to go on a trip with friends because he had a hunting trip planned. I had several negative thoughts that gave me some negative feelings. I knew I was caught up in my thought system, but I didn't get quiet. Instead, I asked Barry, "Would you like to hear my *crazy* thoughts?" (I at least took responsibility for their nature.)

Barry replied good humoredly, "Sure. Go ahead."

I said, "Hunting is more important to you than I am."

Barry calmly replied, "You know that isn't true. I had this planned way ahead. I'll be more than happy to take a trip with you anytime we can find a mutually agreeable time."

I admitted, "I know, but I used to get away with it. I'm just doing my spoiled brat number in which I think the world should revolve around me. I'll get over it soon."

In the past I believed my silly thoughts about hunting being more important than I am. (Actually, so what if it is?) The important difference this time was that I took responsibility for my *crazy* thinking. Even though I felt disappointed, I couldn't take it as seriously as I did when I didn't know I was thinking from my thought system.

My awareness of acting like a spoiled brat made it impossible for those feelings to have much power. It was not long before I could *see* that I didn't need a trip to be happy. I didn't even need to be more important than hunting to be happy.

Intellectual understanding does not change our feelings, but it can help us dismiss our thoughts, or at least take them less seriously, until we have *understanding* from an insight or realization. Our feelings change when understanding comes though our natural state of mind rather than through our thought system.

LISTENING

Whenever we feel upset, we have stopped listening from love and have started listening from ego and a programmed thought system. Using our feeling of being upset is helpful as a compass to let us know we are off track and should start listening deeper.

True listening is forgetting about the details, *hearing* what another person is feeling, and knowing when those feelings are coming from thoughts of insecurity. We recognize the difference from our own feeling level; when we feel love, compassion, or interest rather than judgment or defensiveness, we are listening deeply.

Understanding changes the experience of listening. It is impossible to experience another person's reality, but as soon as we think we can, we have stopped listening and have started dealing with our own experience of what we *think* it is like for them. When we recognize this, it becomes interesting to listen to another person's reality and learn as much as we can. This is possible only when we stop trying to add our own interpretations—when we listen without judgment.

When your partner is upset or caught up in thought, that is the time to *listen,* not to talk. Analyzing does not help. Listening is quietly responding with love and understanding, and when we are in that state of mind our inspiration will let us know exactly how to create positivity—eventually, if not immediately. It might be humor. It might be time alone. It might be a loving touch. It might be a quiet walk. It might be time to rest. We will know.

HAVE FUN TOGETHER

Have you ever noticed that when you are having fun together you are not being judgmental, critical, or dissatisfied? When we want happiness and peace of mind, it makes sense to do things together that bring pleasure and enjoyment.

LIVE IN GRATITUDE

When we dismiss negative thoughts, we are left with feelings of gratitude and appreciation for all that life has to offer. It makes no sense to live in negativity when positivity is just a dropped thought away. When following the treasure map to happiness and peace of mind, *the natural state of a relationship is to enjoy unconditional love.*

117

12

Myths about Relationships

As the following myths are presented, reality is shown to be the opposite of what many of us have been taught all our lives.

MYTH NO. 1: LOVE IS BLIND

Love is not blind. When we are in love we are not blinded by judgments, expectations, and other kinds of filters from our thought system. We *see* differences as interesting, or with understanding and compassion. What other people might see as *faults* in our beloved, we find endearing, we defend, or we brush off as unimportant.

Because Bob promised to call Nancy at 9:30, but didn't until 11:00, she thought he was inconsiderate and uncaring—and told him so. Later, after she realized that when they had fallen in love she had been understanding and compassionate when he called later than promised, it became obvious to her that it wasn't the circumstances, but her thoughts that upset her and created her feelings.

119

When we look through our *judgment glasses,* differences or circumstances are no longer seen with understanding, interest, or compassion. The judgment blinder is so powerful that it can even change what was once seen as a virtue into a "fault."

Marilyn fell in love with Jordan and admired the calm way he drove a car, which made her feel safe and relaxed on rides with him. After they got married, however, she found it often drove her crazy to ride with him because he was unaggressive and didn't take risks to pass slow cars.

Marilyn had also admired Jordan for his quiet, easygoing dependability; he had been in the same job for twelve years, and she could set her clock by his departure and arrival. With her *judgment glasses* on, she started seeing him as boring and lacking ambition. During their courtship she had loved his flexibility and willingness to go along with all her suggestions. Through her judgment blinders, she saw him as spineless and weak, without an original thought in his head.

Marilyn divorced Jordan and married Steve, who was aggressive, ambitious, and opinionated. At first Marilyn admired these "virtues" in Steve and felt lucky to be married to an exciting man who knew what he wanted and where he was going. She felt protected and taken care of. Later, however, she saw him as controlling and unyielding because he would not do what she wanted him to do, and instead of feeling protected, she felt dominated and not taken seriously.

Marilyn divorced Steve and married another man like Jordan. She is now in her seventh marriage because she does not *see* that she loses her good feelings and happiness every time she puts on her blinders of judgment and expectation. She believes she sees reality through her blinders. She is also looking for happiness outside herself and blames others when she doesn't find it there.

Love does not judge differences.

MYTH NO. 2: IT IS IMPORTANT TO BE COMPATIBLE

Dolores divorced Scott. Her explanation: "We just were not compatible." A pervasive distortion of the meaning of compatibility is the notion that two people must have the same beliefs and interests to live together harmoniously.

When we understand separate realities, we can see that it is impossible for two people to be the same. Couples fooled into thinking they have the same interests and beliefs get into trouble when they later find what they thought was the same is not exactly the same.

Dolores and Scott were delighted to discover they both enjoyed tennis. They were already in love, but saw their mutual interest in tennis as proof they were "compatible." The trouble started because Dolores liked to play more often than Scott did, and he thought she took it too seriously. Dolores assumed that anyone really interested in tennis would feel exactly the same way she did about it. They both felt cheated and misunderstood, and the only solution they could see, since they were obviously not as compatible as they thought, was divorce.

Do you find it hard to believe that a couple would

get a divorce because they didn't feel exactly the same about tennis? Any belief about incompatibility makes no more sense than this example.

The true meaning of compatibility is having the ability to live together in harmony. We all have this ability because compatibility is a natural state when we dismiss negative thoughts and respect differences instead of judging them.

Lillian was feeling dissatisfied with Garth because she claimed they had nothing in common. She felt they would both be better off if they broke off their relationship and went their separate ways. Garth felt very hurt and lashed out, "You could not have a long-lasting relationship with anyone!"

Lillian replied indignantly, "How could you say such a stupid thing? I have had friends for years all over the country, even though we don't see each other often. And they are all deep friendships."

The next day Lillian had an insight about why she had such good friendships but usually failed to maintain long-lasting love relationships. She realized that she treated her friends with unconditional love and respect. She never criticized or judged or burdened them with her expectations. When they were down, she encouraged them; when they were up she celebrated with them. Her love relationships started out the same way, but she would soon create thoughts of insecurity that she would try to resolve with expectations, judgments, and criticisms.

As soon as she realized this, she was able to laugh at herself, drop her insecure thoughts, and start treating Garth the way she did her friends. Their love blossomed.

It is unimportant to be compatible in today's commonly defined way; we don't need to have the same interests and beliefs. We have compatibility when we see differences with love, interest, understanding, respect, and acceptance. We are compatible when we are sharing good feelings rather than judgments and expectations. We are naturally compatible when we are experiencing life through our natural state of mind rather than through our thought system.

MYTH NO. 3: IT IS IMPORTANT TO COMMUNICATE ABOUT PROBLEMS

A pervasive distortion also exists of the meaning of communication in relationships. How often have you heard these statements? "We just can't communicate." "The key to a good relationship is communication."

The distortion in these statements is the implied importance of *making* your partner understand and accept what you *feel* and what you *believe*. That is, if you can get your partner to believe your reality rather than his or her own, you have succeeded in "good" communication.

This is the same as saying, "You should have the same reality I have; no more separate reality for you. Also, you should have the same thought system I have, including all my particular judgments, expectations, and desires. You should have my illusions, not your own."

No wonder almost everyone is failing attempts at

good communication. It is impossible for your partner to believe your reality rather than his or her own. With understanding he or she might dismiss both realities for the illusions of thought that they are, but until then he or she "would rather fight than switch."

Because we are always communicating, either from our distorted thought system or from our natural state of mind, knowing where our communication is coming from is important. When we are communicating from our thought system, we are sharing negative feelings, thoughts, and beliefs. Even sulky or angry silences are communication. When we are communicating from our natural state of mind, we are sharing the positive feelings we experience through inspiration, common sense, and wisdom.

Sharing positive feelings is often done silently. Many couples do more quiet touching and less verbal communication when they realize how inadequate words are to express beautiful feelings. When we are in a state of happiness and peace of mind, it is amazing how much we can enjoy what is usually referred to as *mundane* information. "Is dinner ready?" "I paid the bills today." "How are the kids?" "Shall we go to the beach?" Communication becomes light and easy, not heavy in the sense that we communicate "to get it all out" or to make sure our partner knows how we *feel* (from our thought system).

This may sound boring to some people, but happiness and peace of mind are not boring. In that state of mind it is common to feel so full of the joy of living and love for our partners that we sometimes wonder how we can handle it all.

Is another *should* or *shouldn't* creeping into your thoughts? Are you wondering, "Does this mean we shouldn't talk about our separate realities?" What we do is not the point. Talking about our separate realities, or not talking about them, is simply a different experience when we understand the principles. You will probably feel a sense of humor if you do talk about separate realities, instead of taking them seriously.

MYTH NO. 4: NEVER GO TO SLEEP UNTIL YOU HAVE RESOLVED AN ARGUMENT

Sometimes the best way to dismiss thoughts of *right* and *wrong* is some kind of cooling-off period to help us get quiet. This could be sleeping it off, walking around the block, or doing anything else that helps us feel better.

Kate and Frank believed they should never go to sleep until they had resolved their arguments. They would stand toe to toe and argue about who was *right* and who was *wrong*. Since they were both *caught up* in their individual thought systems and separate realities, it was impossible to hear each other or solve anything. Since they believed they *should* be able to solve their arguments, their frustrations would build. Frank would finally leave, slamming the door behind him, and go to the nearest bar. Kate would go to bed, but couldn't sleep because she was furiously thinking about their failure to solve the problem before going to sleep.

After they saw a therapist who taught them about the principles, it became obvious to them what they could do. Frank said to Kate, "Since I like to leave the house when I am upset, I will leave, but I won't slam the door, and I won't go to a bar. I will take a walk around the block until my thought system is tucked away where it can't hurt me, and I am able to enjoy how much I love you again. You can know that my leaving is not anger at you, but just my recognition that I'm *caught up* in my negative thoughts and need to get quiet until they go away."

Kate said, "Since I enjoy relaxing in bed, I will do that. Instead of continuing to think about my negative thoughts, however, I will read a book or go to sleep with the peace-provoking knowledge that they are just thoughts. You can know I'm not going to bed to get away from you, but to rest until the negative thoughts are gone and nothing is left but wisdom and common sense."

MYTH NO. 5: IF YOU ARE NOT HAVING FIGHTS YOU ARE NOT GOING "DEEP" IN YOUR RELATIONSHIP—OR SOMEONE IS GIVING IN TOO MUCH

Couples who understand the principles of psychological functioning that underlie their separate realities do not fight, or at least realize they are off track when they do.

Sylvia shared, "I can't remember the last time Tim and I had a fight. It has been at least four years. We had lots of fights before, but now we just enjoy each other."

Scott shared, "Lisa and I still have fights, but they are all silent. We know that if we feel like fighting we are just in a low mood, or lost in our thought systems, so we keep quiet and wait for it to pass."

Beth shared, "Tom and I used to have fights and

lose respect for each other. We still have fights once in a while, but now we lose respect for the fights instead of for each other."

Kathie shared, "When Dave and I have fights now, we seldom take them seriously for long, so we end up laughing. It is especially fun to watch my 'Sarah Bernhardt' act while I am still taking things a little bit seriously."

I used to get upset when I wanted to "discuss" something with my husband, and he would tell me, "Forget it." I would retort, "What do you mean, 'forget it'? If you had any sensitivity at all, you would be upset too." Now I say, "Thanks for reminding me."

MYTH NO. 6: WE WILL BE HAPPY WHEN OUR CIRCUMSTANCES CHANGE

Happiness is a state of mind that has nothing to do with circumstances. "Dear Abby" received a letter from a woman complaining about her husband's snoring. "Dear Abby" included another letter from a woman who stated, "I used to complain about snoring. My husband is dead now. I would give anything to be able to hear him snoring again."

An often-told story is the one about struggling new-lyweds who do not appreciate the joy of being together and in love because they keep focusing on how much better it will be when they have more money, a house, and furniture. Then they get the money, house, and furniture, but don't enjoy them because they think they are not as much in love as they used to be. In fact they do not experience the love because they keep focusing on circumstances and miss the joy of *what is*. They cannot see *what is* when focusing on *what is not*.

We feel dissatisfaction in a relationship when we are focusing on what we think we *should* be getting to satisfy our beliefs about how things *should* be. When we recognize what we are doing to create this dissatisfaction, we can see that these beliefs are always connected to our illusionary ego and self-importance.

We have satisfaction, peace of mind, and happiness in our relationships when we are loving unconditionally—when we take off our blinders and see our partner the same way we did when we fell in love. You might object, "But my wife is not the same as when we fell in love. She wasn't fat then." The answer to every objection you might have can be found in the principles. Your happiness has nothing to do with what anyone else is or does. If you are seeing the fat, you are not seeing the insecurity, which you may have helped create. *When you see with LOVE instead of with JUDGMENT, you will also see solutions.*

June was miserable because her husband, Cy, was an alcoholic. She vowed to herself that if he did not stop drinking by the time the children left home, she would leave him. They had been married thirty years when the last child left for college. Before June kept her vow, she decided to see a therapist, who taught her the principles. She was surprised at the clear inspiration she received from her inner wisdom: "It is not your province to judge your husband, but to love him unconditionally." June's reality changed; she loved Cy unconditionally without effort, and within three months he stopped drinking.

Some people have interpreted this story to mean that a woman should deny the problems of alcoholism and become an enabler by ignoring the issue.

If you have heard the principles with understanding you realize that the story does not mean anything except what happened to one woman who listened to the inspiration from her inner wisdom. Someone else might hear a totally different message. The message could be to leave with love or to lovingly insist on an intervention program. The possibilities are limitless. Only one thing will always be the same—positive results are experienced when following our inner wisdom.

MYTH NO. 7: WHEN YOU LOVE SOMEONE, IT IS NATURAL TO FEEL INSECURE; JEALOUSY IS A SIGN THAT YOU CARE

Jealousy is created from the ego and is based on the notion that possessiveness will cure feelings of inadequacy. It is a subtle way of trying to get someone else to take responsibility for our own happiness.

Jealousy is just insecurity produced by thoughts about ego and self-importance, which is based on a fear of being unimportant. These insecurities usually take some form of vulnerability fear: fear of inadequacy, fear of rejection, or fear of powerlessness.

These fears are merely illusions based on taking thoughts of ego and self-importance seriously. Yet many people base their lives on these illusions, wasting time and energy trying to hide their fears, or trying to blame themselves or others as the cause of their fears.

Fears of inadequacy take such forms as, "I won't be

good enough. Someone else will be better than I am. If only I were more beautiful, more handsome, more powerful, more successful, more intelligent, more witty; then I would be okay."

Fears of rejection take such forms as, "He won't care as much as I care, which means I'm not good enough, which means he might leave me, which means I will be alone and will never find anyone else."

Fears of powerlessness take such forms as, "I can't do anything about this. I have no control over what is happening to me. I can't make someone love me."

Self-esteem is a natural state of being when it is not weighted down with thoughts that produce the illusion of insecurity. The following poem illustrates the kind of crazy thoughts and feelings that can be produced when taking thoughts of insecurity seriously.

Self-Esteem
Self-esteem—
    such an elusive concept.

Understanding it
    intellectually
    is not so difficult.

Of course I'm okay
    just as I am.
Certainly it doesn't matter
    what anyone else thinks.

Then why do I feel
    this pit
    in my stomach
when I think

you might not care
enough?
   (What is enough?)

Why am I afraid
to care
  too much?
    (What is too much?)

For fear
you might not care
  as much.
    (What is as much?)

Of course, self-esteem is an elusive concept—an illusion based on the illusion of ego. How could you lack self-esteem without THINKING you have no self-esteem? Then can you imagine trying to build self-esteem, working from a premise that you don't have it? The belief that anyone can lack self-worth is an extremely silly thought. When seen as reality, however, the illusions created by silly thoughts are powerful detours away from happiness.

Bill and Sue went to a party. When Bill saw Sue dancing with another man he became angry and sulked on the way home until Sue persuaded him to admit something was wrong. Then he blew! He blamed her for flirting and accused her of being inconsiderate. He would not accept her explanation that she didn't even want to dance with the other man, but didn't know how to refuse gracefully.

Bill had become so lost in the contents of his thinking that he didn't connect his behavior with his original

131

thoughts of insecurity. He had used blame to cover up his thoughts of vulnerability fears, which were that Sue might find him inadequate compared with the other man and that she might decide to reject him, against which he felt powerless. Expressing anger gave him a false sense of power and control—not happiness.

Bill decided to leave Sue, to protect himself from being left by her. Bill's thinking is illustrated in the following poem.

Perpetuation
I keep worrying
that you
will reject me.

That would be
   terrible
     because
       I love being with you.

Isn't it crazy
that to keep you
from rejecting me
   I get defensive (offensive)
     and reject you?

So
I save myself
from possible rejection
   but the results
   are the same:
     I can't be with you.

And

it is
terrible!

Is that called
perpetuating
what you fear?

Insecurity has nothing to do with reality, but
instead is based on negative thoughts seen as reality.
Look at the unhappiness Bill created when he took his
thoughts seriously. For some crazy thoughts, he gave up
his happiness.

It would have been much simpler for Bill to dismiss
his negative thoughts instead of dismissing his marriage.

MYTH NO. 8: YOU HAVE
TO HAVE A RELATIONSHIP

Who says you have to have a relationship?

This myth is just another belief based on another
thought, and when you look at the evidence, it makes
no sense. There are just as many (or more) unhappy
people in relationships as there are happy people in
relationships. In fact, there are just as many people who
are happy even though they don't have a relationship, as
there are people who are unhappy *because they don't
have a relationship.*

It is all thought, not circumstance. When we have
peace of mind, gratitude, and satisfaction with all that *IS,*
we don't see *what is not.* We are happy with or without
a relationship.

We can be in love with life, alone.

13

Children

All parents chuckle and feel a bond when they hear, "Aren't children wonderful—when they are asleep?" *Understanding* will help you *see* your children as wonderful most of the time. When you don't see them as wonderful, you will know it is not that they are less than wonderful, but that you are caught up in your thought system.

I have written a book entitled *Positive Discipline,* * which is full of common sense and wisdom for working with children in effective and loving ways. Before understanding the principles of psychological functioning, I often turned the common sense and wisdom into rules and *shoulds,* and felt like a failure when I did not follow them.

* Jane Nelsen, *Positive Discipline* (New York: Ballantine, 1987). Available from Sunrise Press (1-800-456-7770).

The *understanding* I now have makes it easier to *see* the principle and deeper wisdom behind each suggestion in *Positive Discipline*. From a happy state of mind, following these suggestions is natural rather than difficult. When I don't follow common sense and wisdom, I forgive myself, learn from my mistakes, and clean up the mess I created from using my thought system. Some of the information in this chapter and the next is adapted from *Positive Discipline*.

EXAMPLE IS THE BEST TEACHER

Have you ever noticed how many *unhappy* parents are telling their children what they *should* do to be successful and happy? These parents are often filled with stress, anxiety, and other forms of thought-produced insecurity because they follow false premises from their thought systems for finding happiness outside themselves.

If they took a close look at their own lives, a lot of parents would *see* why so many children are rebelling today. By the time children become teenagers, they begin to see discrepancies between what we say and how we live. They see parents who live in unhappiness and other forms of dissatisfaction as they try to *prove themselves* based on society's notions of success. No wonder teenagers have little respect for the establishment.

When we take a closer look, it becomes obvious that success has become more important than happiness and serenity. In fact, happiness is often sacrificed for the illusion of success. At a deep *feeling* level, many teenagers know this makes no sense, and they rebel. Their rebellion, however, is often based on thoughts that create other forms of insecurity, and consequently they choose a lifestyle that brings no greater happiness than that of their parents. Other teenagers conform and join in the illusion of trying to live up to society's notions of success.

Children will find their own sanity when they experience sanity from their parents. When they experience insanity (crazy thinking) from their parents, they seem to prefer their own insanity. Unfortunately, far too many adopt the insanity of their parents and pass it on to the next generation.

With *understanding,* parents can live a truly happy life. They can create an atmosphere of common sense and wisdom and be models their children will want to follow. When we become happy people, our children are more likely to become happy people. When we follow common sense and wisdom, our children will follow common sense and wisdom. This does not mean we will live in bliss all the time, because it is too easy to succumb to the world's seductions and the habit of following our illusionary egos and thought systems. Understanding the principles acts as a reliable road map to help us find our way back to serenity whenever we get tired of the misery we create.

FEEDING FIRES

Children often start harmless little fires that would quickly burn out if adults didn't feed the flames until they became roaring bonfires.

Every Christmas after all the presents have been opened my children complain, "Is that all?"

My thoughts used to go crazy over issues of selfishness, lack of gratitude, and spoiled bratness, and I would start my lecture, "It doesn't matter how much we do for you kids, it is never enough. Next Christmas everyone is going to get one present, period, and we'll spend the rest of the day in an orphanage so you can see what it is like to have nothing." We would all end up feeling bad about Christmas and each other.

Last Christmas when I heard, "Is that all?" I replied, "I can remember having that feeling when I was a little girl."

There was an incredulous, "Really? Then how come you call us spoiled when we say it?"

I answered, "Temporary insanity." The children laughed and went off to enjoy their new possessions.

A friend recently shared that she once had the same problem. (This type of thing goes on in thousands of households.) She said, "Last Christmas I ignored the remark (did not feed the flame) and noticed only seconds later that my little girl, acting as if she had never felt any disappointment, was playing with her toys."

IN THE BEGINNING

Babies come into this world with their natural states of mind unblocked by thought systems. They have neither memories of the past, nor thoughts of the future; they smile when they are happy and cry when they want something; they are curious, giving their full attention to whatever they are interested in; they stare, without embarrassment, at anything or anyone new; they have natural learning abilities and easily learn a language and many other things without *thinking* about it.

Toddlers are not worried about making mistakes while learning to walk. Can you imagine what would happen if they had negative thoughts every time they fell down? The first thing most of them would "think" is that they could not possibly accomplish these great tasks of walking and talking, and their progress would stop. They don't think those kinds of thoughts until adults start feeding them negative beliefs. We fail to follow our inner wisdom and inspiration and prevent our children from following theirs. Instead, we teach them all kinds of behavioral rules, along with the crazy idea that self-worth depends on how well they obey those rules.

It may sound as if I am advocating permissiveness. Following inspiration (which will let us know exactly how much guidance our children need and how to do it), and allowing children to do the same, is nothing like permissiveness. Children often lose access to their natural state of mind because they love us so much they accept what we tell them, whether or not it comes from our natural state of mind.

YES OR NO

When coming from inspiration, we know which answer is appropriate to our children's requests. I used to say yes out of guilt, or no out of insecurity. In other words, the basis for my answers would be something like, "I should say yes to make up for past neglect. I should say yes or they might get mad at me. I had better say yes because I can't handle the hassle right now. I have to say no or they might get spoiled. I have to say no because they might take advantage of me if I say yes. I had better say no or they will expect yes all the time."

It is amazing how little my children hassle me when I follow inspiration from my natural state of mind before answering yes or no. I have noticed I don't say no because of some future possibility as often. And when I do say no, it is with a feeling of love and sometimes humor, and it is accepted in the same spirit.

LISTEN DEEPLY

If we are hearing something from our children that makes us feel upset, we are not listening deeply enough. We are reacting (from ego) to the words rather than to the insecurity behind the words. When we hear the feeling level, we will be inspired to respond lovingly.

The minute I returned home from a few days' absence recently, Mary started barraging me with, "Take me here. Take me there." I wanted to let her know how unrealistic she was being, that I was tired, that all she cared about was what I could *do* for her instead of being glad to see me, and that she needed to be more considerate.

Then I started listening deeper and could see that she just wanted to be with me. I said, "Let's sit down and plan something we can do together at a time convenient for both of us." Mary immediately calmed down.

MISTAKES

Mistakes do not matter; they are simply opportunities to learn. So what if we think a negative thought and act on it? So what if we get into a low mood and yell at our children? Recovery is just an insight away. Getting off track is nothing to get upset about when we know what causes it and what to do about it. I call this recovery.

RECOVERY

Mrs. Lamont tells how she used recovery after dealing with a situation brought on by craziness. She found a six-pack of beer in fourteen-year-old Marie's closet. When Marie came home, she was met at the door by her mother, beer in hand, who demanded in an accusing voice, "What is this?"

Marie sarcastically replied, "It looks like a six-pack of beer to me."

Mrs. Lamont snapped back, "Don't get smart with me, young lady. I found this in the bottom of your closet."

Marie remembered, "Oh, I had forgotten all about that. I was hiding it for a friend."

"Do you expect me to believe that?"

"I don't care if you believe it or not," Marie shouted as she ran to her room.

Mrs. Lamont called after her, "You are grounded for a week, Miss Smart Mouth."

Mrs. Lamont shared this incident with her friend Lillian, who helped her get back in touch with her common sense by asking, "Why were you upset about the beer?"

Mrs. Lamont (still caught up in her thought system) indignantly replied, "Because I don't want her to get into trouble."

Lillian could see that her friend had still lost sight of her common sense, and gently prodded, "And why don't you want her to get into trouble?"

Mrs. Lamont thought Lillian must really be dense as she replied with exasperation, "Because I don't want her to ruin her life!"

Lillian continued, "And why don't you want her to ruin her life?"

Mrs. Lamont finally understood and replied sheepishly, "You mean because I love her. I can see now that I did not let that message get through. Thanks, Lillian. I know what to do now."

That evening Mrs. Lamont sat down with Marie, saying, "I'm sorry for the way I acted yesterday. I said some pretty silly things."

"That's okay, Mom. I really was hiding it for a friend."

"Marie, I love you. Sometimes I get scared when I have thoughts that you might hurt yourself. Then I forget to tell you I love you and just blurt out my craziness."

Marie started to cry and said, "I have been feeling that I was just a big problem to you and that only my friends like me."

"I can see how you could get that impression from my behavior. Can we start over?"

Mrs. Lamont finished her story, "I don't know if

Marie will drink beer or not, but I know I am not now increasing the chance that she will because of the insecurity she feels about our relationship. We now have regular family meetings (we are a family of two) and work out solutions with love."

Children are so forgiving. They may be feeling resentment or rebellion when we are humiliating them, but as soon as we say we are sorry they are quick to say, "That's okay." Recovery can be a beautiful way to make a relationship even nicer than it was before. Recovery is natural when we dismiss negative thoughts and *see* the situation with new perspective.

ENJOYING CHILDREN

I have a great idea for a book on child rearing, with a guarantee that would make it a best-seller: If you don't experience wonderful results *after following the advice* in this $10 book for one year, you will receive 100 times your money back. In other words, satisfaction or $1,000. (This guarantee is backed by Lloyd's of London.)

I think people would be stampeding the bookstores—even after they learned that the book contained only three words. Would you like to know what those three words would be?

Enjoy your children.

When we are enjoying our children, we will experience fantastic results in all areas of child rearing. What to do to achieve positive results will be natural and easy from this state of mind, even though *what to do* may be different for each parent.

When children fight, one parent may join them in a

good-natured wrestling match. Another parent may say, "This doesn't look like fun to me. I think I'll take a walk around the block until you are finished." Another parent may lose his or her happy state of mind and punish the children, and then use *recovery* as soon as he or she regains a happy state of mind. Another parent may send the children to their rooms, telling them to come out only when they are ready to hold a "peace conference." Another parent may say, "Here are the boxing gloves. The fight area is outside." The possibilities for every situation are unlimited when you enjoy your children and follow the inspiration from your natural state of mind.

When we are following the inspiration from our natural state of mind, it is natural to love and enjoy our children and to know what to do when they need guidance. When children experience this kind of atmosphere, they are less likely to go wrong. Although they will probably still establish a thought system, and sometimes get caught up in it and do things that don't produce positive results, they have learned from us how to get back on course to lead a happy life.

Provide a good feeling level, and all problems will take care of themselves. This does not mean you will never have to do anything. It means that when you are feeling good, you will know what to do for positive results.

14

Myths of Child Rearing

Well-meaning efforts have created some interesting myths regarding the best way to help children achieve success and happiness.

MYTH NO. 1: PUNISHMENT TEACHES CHILDREN TO IMPROVE THEIR BEHAVIOR

Wherever did we get the crazy idea that in order to make children do better, we first have to make them feel worse? Making children feel bad lowers their mood, or level of consciousness, so they don't behave better. They behave better when they feel good.

Parents punish their children because of thought-created insecurity in the form of fear of failure (their children's and their own), a mistaken belief that punishment will help, and blocked access to inspiration from their inner wisdom.

Punishment comes from a lower level of consciousness, thought-system beliefs, and lack of respect for separate realities. Children usually react to punishment with one of the following forms of their own thought systems:

1. Resentment ("This is unfair.")
2. Revenge ("They are winning now, but I'll get even.")
3. Rebellion ("I'll do just the opposite of what they want.")
4. Retreat:
   a. Sneakiness ("I won't get caught next time.")
   b. Insecurity ("I am a bad person.")

Punishment is one way we teach children to program their thought systems and to live from that source, rather than from their natural state of mind.

Children who are punished do not come to their parents when they have questions about life. Children do come to parents who interact with them from inspiration and wisdom. Parents who interact with their children from their natural state of mind will know what to do to teach their children with love, understanding, and compassion.

MYTH NO. 2: CHILDREN NEED TO LEARN OBEDIENCE

Children will not be helped by learning obedience, but rather by learning to follow the inspiration from their inner wisdom and common sense, which will never lead them astray.

When they are babies, they need supervision and

guidance, which is different from obedience. Supervision and guidance are based on feelings of love and concern for the safety and well-being of our children. When parents stay in touch with their inner wisdom and common sense, they will know how to guide their children in ways that will achieve positive results. When children experience examples of common sense and wisdom, they will follow them when they grow beyond the need for guidance and supervision.

A toddler has neither enough information and understanding to stay out of the path of moving cars, nor the capability to understand obedience about that.

Parents often insist they must spank their children to teach them obedience about staying out of the street. I ask these parents, "After you have given your children a spanking for running into the street, do you let them play by themselves near a busy street?" I have never found a parent who said yes; they all agree that they need to supervise their children near busy streets until they are five or six. Punishment does not help children stay out of the street.

Teaching children to look both ways to see if a car is coming before crossing a street gives them both needed supervision while they are young and common-sense information they can rely on when they are more mature. They still need supervision until they are five or six.

Not teaching obedience does not mean being permissive. Many families teach common-sense responsibility and cooperation by having family meetings in which the children take part in handling most potential problem situations, such as chores, homework, and dis-

147

agreements. These families work together to under-stand and respect separate realities, and to decide on solutions that make sense to everyone.

Instead of teaching obedience, use and teach reliance on inner wisdom and inspiration.

MYTH NO. 3: BE A PARENT, NOT A FRIEND, TO YOUR CHILDREN

I am unsure what being a parent and not a friend means, but it makes parenting sound like an unfriendly chore in which you must remain superior and aloof. I have heard parents talk about how important it is to maintain authority and control. Mutual respect, cooperation, and shared responsibility are much more effective.

It can be such fun to share life with children, so it makes no sense not to enjoy them as we discover who they are. Unfortunately, parents often tell their children who they should be, instead of discovering and enjoying who they are.

One reason we enjoy being around friends is because they love us unconditionally. They are usually very good at helping us see things from common sense and wisdom instead of from our programmed thought system, so just being around a friend can raise our mood, or level of consciousness.

There need not be any difference between being a parent and being a friend. Children want and appreciate advice when it comes from common sense and wisdom, but they are confused or rebellious when advice comes from a thought system. Just as our friends do, they want unconditional love and acceptance, not judgment.

Children will learn more from us when we interact with them the way we do with friends.

MYTH NO. 4: PROBLEMS MUST BE DEALT WITH IMMEDIATELY

Use your feelings as a compass to let you know when to deal with a problem. If you are upset, you know you are *caught up* in your thought system, and nothing you do from that state of mind will achieve positive results. It is often helpful to let your children know you need *time out* or a cooling-off period before you can talk about the situation.

Mr. Stewart had an interesting way of calling for time out. He would exaggerate his feelings and jokingly say to his son, Andrew, "If you don't run, I'll probably clobber you."

Andrew would run. When they both felt better, after a cooling-off period, they would get back together and solve the problem with good feelings.

Understanding helps us know when we are in a low mood, and to dismiss our thoughts and be quiet until it passes. When we forget, and do something with our children that doesn't feel good, it can always be *fixed* through *recovery* when we are in a better mood.

MYTH NO. 5: WHAT OTHER PEOPLE THINK ABOUT YOUR PARENTING SKILLS IS IMPORTANT

I remember claiming once that to be a good mother was one of the most important things in life to me. A wise and observant friend asked, "In whose eyes? The neighbors' or your children's?"

The question hit me hard as I realized how much what I did as a mother was to seek approval from others. With that as a motive, I could not follow my inner inspiration to get the best results with my children.

Social pressure is just another illusion; it cannot hurt us unless we take it seriously. Wanting to live up to our imagined expectations of others is an *ego trip* that will definitely interfere with inner wisdom and inspiration.

One summer, when Mark was ten years old, we went backpacking with several friends. Mark was a good sport and carried his pack the long, six miles into the canyon. As we were getting ready for the steep return trek, Mark complained that his pack was uncomfortable.

His dad jokingly remarked, "You can take it. You're the son of a marine."

Mark did not think that was very funny, since it did not solve his problem, but he started the climb anyway. He had gone only a little ahead of us when we heard his pack crashing down the hill.

I thought he had fallen and called out, "Mark! Are you okay? What happened?"

Mark angrily called back, "Nothing; it hurts!" He continued climbing without his pack.

The rest of the group watched with interest. One adult offered to carry his pack for him.

My thoughts went crazy: "What are people going to think? They are all wondering if I can make *Positive Discipline* work. What if I can't? They will think I'm terrible if I just let Mark *get away* with that."

I dismissed those thoughts and remembered I was more interested in Mark than in what other people thought.

I asked the rest of the party to hike on ahead so we could handle this in private. I then did the best I could to understand Mark's reality and asked, "Did you think we didn't care because we didn't pay serious attention when you tried to tell us your pack hurt before we even started?"

Mark replied, "Yes, and I'm not going to carry it."

His dad said, "I'm sorry, son, can we start over?"

Mark agreed, and they figured out a way to stuff his coat over the sore part to cushion the pack. Mark carried the pack the rest of the way with only a few, minor complaints.

We have found that our children always respond positively to sanity and are very forgiving and cooperative when we recognize we have made a mistake and follow our inner wisdom to correct it.

MYTH NO. 6: CHILDREN SHOULD BE SEEN AND NOT HEARD

That children should be seen and not heard may sound like an old-fashioned myth that is not prevalent today. We claim to care about what children have to say, but how often do we really hear and *understand* the separate realities of our children? How often do we punish first and ask questions later?

When Kenny was seven, Bradley five, and Lisa three, my husband and I took them with us while looking at building lots. Bradley and Kenny complained the whole time about how hot and boring it was. Lisa played quietly on my lap or took a nap.

Because we wanted to continue our search the next day, we thought we would be doing Kenny and Bradley a big favor by leaving them with the neighbors who had children their ages. We planned to take Lisa with us because she had not been a problem.

When we started to leave, Kenny said, "I want to go."

I replied, "No you don't. Remember how much you complained about how hot and boring it was yesterday?"

Kenny said, "I don't care. I want to go."

I insisted that he did not really want to go, and we left without him.

When we returned home we saw that he had taken a knife and slashed the material on Lisa's high chair. I spanked him and sent him to his room.

In a few hours, when I was in a better mood and able to guess what Kenny might have been thinking, I went into his room and checked it out with him. "Kenny, did you think that because we took Lisa with us, and not you, that we loved her more than we love you?"

"Yes," Kenny sobbed.

I shared, "I can guess what that felt like, because I had a similar thing happen to me. When I was ten, my mother took my older sister to New York City. She said I couldn't go because I was not old enough, but I thought it was because she loved my sister more than me."

Kenny responded, "Really?"

I asked, "Would you like to know how I felt about not taking you with us?"

Kenny nodded, so I proceeded, "I love you very much. I didn't want you to be hot and bored. I thought you would have much more fun playing with your friends than being cooped up in the car."

He grinned happily. Kenny could now hear my reality after I had really heard his reality.

I went on, "Now we need to do something about the high chair. Do you have any ideas?"

Kenny enthusiastically claimed, "I can fix it!"

I agreed, "I'll bet you can."

Kenny took fifty cents from his allowance. We went to a store, found a remnant, and stapled a new covering on the high chair. The high chair was better than brand new, and so was our relationship.

You could call this *recovery*, as explained in the last chapter, but be careful about looking at anything as a technique. It was simply the result of *understanding* that came from dismissing negative thoughts, allowing my level of consciousness to be raised so I could see the situation with perspective. When we try to turn a principle into a technique we take the heart out of it, which is why techniques usually fall flat and do not really work.

From a higher level of consciousness, we know through inspiration what to do to create feelings of love and understanding. With love and understanding, problems are solved, and we enjoy beautiful relationships with our children.

15

Wisdom, and Lack of Wisdom, from the Ages

Wisdom from the ages makes sense at a deeper level when we understand the principles of thinking as a function, separate realities, levels of consciousness, and feelings as a compass.

IF YOU CAN'T SAY SOMETHING NICE, DON'T SAY ANYTHING AT ALL

It is easy to *see* the wisdom in saying nothing if it isn't nice when we know our reality is just a creation of our thoughts, rather than *the only* reality. It makes no sense to say something nasty or judgmental about other realities. Since negative feelings are simply an indicator of a low mood and not seeing things with perspective and understanding, it is wise not to say anything at all during that time.

As soon as we dismiss our negative thoughts, seeing or saying something unkind will not be part of our reality.

COUNT TO TEN

Counting to ten is just another way of dismissing thought and getting quiet until low moods pass. Some of us may need to count to ten thousand before we *see* with clarity and perspective.

HASTE MAKES WASTE

The concept of haste making waste makes sense when we know that the need to hurry to figure things out keeps us bogged down in our thought systems. We gain perspective when we slow down and leave room for inspiration.

STICKS AND STONES CAN BREAK MY BONES, BUT NAMES WILL NEVER HURT ME

Shari said, "I feel like a failure because my husband tells me I never do anything right. No wonder I don't have any self-esteem."

Shari's feelings have nothing to do with what her husband says; instead, it is her thoughts about what he says that create her feelings. If Shari would dismiss her thoughts about what her husband says, she would *see* with perspective and *understand* that what he says comes from his separate reality. She would *see* the innocence and insecurity behind what he is saying. If he had understanding he would not have negative feelings and perceptions that he feels he needs to express.

With *understanding* Shari would know what to do. Instead of taking his thoughts seriously, she could let them pass *right over her thought system.* She might then feel inspired to hug him, make a joke, take a walk, or whatever her common sense would lead her to do.

A STITCH IN TIME SAVES NINE

The only stitch we need to take is to *understand* thought, and the trouble this will save us is greater than nine.

A small tear in cloth gets larger and larger unless it is stitched while it is still small. In the same way, a negative thought can get more and more powerful unless it is dismissed as soon as you *realize* it is just a thought.

There is also an interesting difference: when you let a tear in cloth get larger it takes more work to fix it, but it is as simple to dismiss thoughts that have run rampant for years as it is to dismiss so-called less important thoughts. As soon as you recognize a thought for what it is, the negative power is gone.

An understanding of the principles also helps us *see* the lack of wisdom in some of the old adages.

IDLENESS IS THE DEVIL'S WORKSHOP

Idleness is not a sin; it leaves room for inspiration. Nevertheless, so many people fear that if they are not constantly *busy* they will not be productive.

What is *productiveness?* Productivity from inspiration produces happiness; productivity from the thought system produces unhappiness. We may be productive in achievement, financial success, or a spotless house, while our personal or family life is falling apart. Or we may be productive trying to find satisfaction outside ourselves and wonder why we can't become satisfied.

Wayne Dyer tells a wonderful story in his tape series, "Secrets of the Universe."* Once there were two alley cats. The young cat spent his days frantically chasing his tail. One day the old alley cat wandered by and stopped to watch the young cat. He finally interrupted and asked, "Would you mind telling me what you are doing?"

The young alley cat stopped, took a few minutes to catch his breath, and explained, "I went to cat philosophy school and learned that happiness is in the end of our tails. I know that if I chase long enough and hard enough, I am going to catch a big bite of that happiness."

The old alley cat reflected, "I have not been to cat philosophy school, but I know it is true that happiness is in the end of our tails. I have observed, however, that if I simply wander around enjoying my life, it follows me everywhere I go."

The way some of us run around in circles trying to be "productive" could be seen as trying to catch a big bite of that happiness somewhere outside ourselves. We could learn much from the wise old alley cat.

Actually, it is never what we do that matters, but why we do it, and the results we achieve. When we are

* Nightingale Conant Corp., The Human Resources Company,® Chicago, IL.

idle because we are happy and want to just enjoy life, we will find more happiness. When we are idle because we are unhappy (depressed or bored), we become more unhappy.

It is a popular opinion today that watching television is a waste of time. Maybe so, maybe not. We can watch television as part of our enjoyment of life, or as an effort to escape life. We can avoid watching television because we are afraid of what other people will think (instead of trusting our own wisdom), or because we have adopted the belief that "only uneducated people who don't have anything better to do watch television."

The same could be said of any activity or inactivity in life. When achieving happiness and peace of mind is our only goal, we will know what to do regardless of what anyone else has ever thought or said.

THE ROAD TO HELL IS PAVED WITH GOOD INTENTIONS

We all have good intentions to be happy and do the best we can based on our present level of understanding.

Forgiveness is easy when we *understand* the good intentions of ourselves and others, difficult when we pay attention to the behavior resulting from the insecurities produced by a distorted thought system. The thought system distorts good intentions and can interpret happiness as money, possessions, fame, power, or anything outside oneself.

People locked into their thought system and negative behavior have created a kind of hell. It is our judgments of them that lead to our own kind of hell.

A PERSON WITHOUT GOALS IS LIKE A SHIP WITHOUT A RUDDER

A person with goals is like a boat not without a rudder but with a rudder stuck in one position. Being without goals allows us to enjoy opportunities as they come along.

The belief that we must have goals is based on thoughts that create insecurity, such as "Without goals we will never accomplish anything." People who have goals based on those thoughts do not accomplish happiness; instead, because they often reach their goals and quickly invent new ones so they won't feel useless if not accomplishing something, they feel only temporary satisfaction.

When we are not focused on *goals* for the sake of achievement, we will see *opportunities* for the sake of enjoyment. Productivity is enhanced through enjoyment. With understanding we want to accomplish only the things that are enhancing, rather than to accomplish those things that satisfy our illusionary ego or to live up to the judgments of others.

This is why New Year's resolutions so often fail after a brief spurt of success; we have taken a goal and put it outside ourselves. Successful resolutions have stayed inside where they feed on the energy of inspiration.

We often look at someone who is accomplishing something and say, "Wow, she really has self-discipline and sticks to her goals." If you take a closer look you will often find that she is not following a goal, but is following inspiration. Inspiration provides energy; goals placed outside ourselves drain energy. It is difficult not to follow inspiration, but it is difficult to muster the energy to pursue a goal. Setting up an external goal is taking something that flows naturally (inspiration) and mistaking it for a technique.

ANYTHING WORTH DOING
IS WORTH DOING WELL

The maxim "Anything worth doing is worth doing well" could be true if "well" simply means that you enjoy doing it, but "well" is usually a judgment, with implications of perfection. Beliefs about perfection often take the joy out of doing.

How many people will not sing for the fun of it because they feel they can not sing well enough? This is just one example of the many things people will not do for the pleasure of the doing because of the fear of not living up to the judgment of doing it "well."

Anything worth doing is worth doing for the fun of it!

GROWTH IS PAINFUL

It is true that what is referred to as *growth* within the thought system is painful. Coping is stressful, but it is seen as growth. Delving into the past, expressing *feelings* or anger, overcoming *obstacles,* and controlling *emotions,* are the kinds of "growth that can be very painful." The pain is unnecessary.

Growth based on inspiration from common sense and wisdom is not painful. It is painless to dismiss thoughts upon which the pain is based.

161

We are completely satisfied when we *see* life with *understanding,* but it keeps getting better because our understanding continues to grow and deepen. There is nothing painful about it.

IT'S TOO GOOD TO BE TRUE

The only thing that can take away the goodness in something is negative thoughts. Think it, and you have it. If you think the goodness can't last, you have already started to create misery instead of enjoying what is.

If we think something can't last, it is because we have quit enjoying what is and have adopted thoughts such as, "I can't be happy if I don't have this," or, "It might not last," or, "I don't deserve it."

It is true that "it" might not last. So what? Becoming attached to "it" just keeps you from seeing so much more.

GOOD THINGS ALWAYS COME TO AN END

When we think, "Good things always come to an end," we have put on our blinders so we can't *see* the abundance of good things. Good things don't come to an end until we change our thoughts and start worrying about the past or future and stop enjoying what is. When we *see* the abundance of good things, it makes no sense to worry about losing one good thing.

From our natural state of mind we will *see* WHAT IS with gratitude. There is always something to be grateful for.

Life is good.

16

Keys to Happiness—
A Summary

Would you like to be in prison? Would you knowingly confine yourself to a lifetime sentence in a dungeon? Although you may think these are ridiculous questions, you may have locked yourself in a prison without realizing what you have done. You may feel the confinement of the life you have created without being aware that it is totally your creation.

Your thought system creates a prison more confining than any dungeon. The prison walls you create in your mind are formed from illusionary thoughts, but they can be as binding as concrete.

The foundation stones for an illusionary but confining prison are made of thoughts that create feelings of insecurity. The walls of the prison are made of whatever form the insecurity takes—self-importance, drinking, anxiety, overeating, judgment, overachievement,

163

expectation, stress, dissatisfaction, depression, blame. The ceiling is the belief that these thoughts are reality.

THE PRINCIPLES AS KEYS TO HAPPINESS

An understanding of the principles we have discussed in previous chapters is the master key to the prison doors. Know the truth, and the truth shall make you free.

There can be a wide chasm, however, between intellectual knowledge and experiential reality. Intellectually I believed that happiness came from within, but I did not understand the barriers that kept me from experiencing the truth of that knowledge. An understanding of the four principles provided the treasure map that led me past the barriers to my inner happiness.

Thinking as a Function

The foundation principle is *realizing* that thinking is a function. This realization is the key to experiencing natural mental health and inner happiness. Those who believe the contents of their thinking reflect an external reality and often experience stress, anxiety, and other forms of insecurity. They take negative thoughts seriously, turn them into beliefs, and live for them. They have created a prison.

Those who *understand* that thinking is a function (and know they can think anything they want) experience freedom and serenity. By seeing the humor in their negative creations and not taking them seriously, they are able to dismiss negativity and experience natural well-being. They have unlocked the prison doors.

Feelings as a Compass

The principle of using our feelings as a compass is the tool that lets us know where we are on our treasure map. Anytime we are feeling bad, we have forgotten that thinking is a function, and we therefore see our thoughts as reality. Anytime we are feeling good, the treasure is no longer buried; we are living from our natural state of mind and inner happiness.

Separate Realities

When we *understand* the principle of separate realities we see differences with interest and compassion rather than with judgment. We often ignore the fact that we have made ourselves miserable with our judgments and forget that serenity is just a dropped thought away. When we see others with interest and compassion, it is because we are experiencing life from our natural state of mind and inner happiness.

Mood Levels

The principle of mood levels, or levels of consciousness, is closely related to the rest. We are in a low mood, or level of consciousness, when we forget that thinking is a function, when we forget to respect separate realities, when we forget to use our compass as a guide, and especially when we try to use our thought system to find a solution to our predicament. An *understanding* of this principle implies a higher level of consciousness, which will lead us to compassion for ourselves while we wait for a low mood to pass.

BARRIERS TO HAPPINESS

Between intellectual knowledge and experiential understanding of the principles, however, are barriers, created in our thought system, that can keep us from our inner happiness and serenity.

Circumstances

It is never the circumstances, but only our thoughts about circumstances that create our state of mind. We can always find examples of people who have maintained their peace of mind under the same circumstances we *think* are causing us to feel awful, and many books could be, and have been, written about their inspiring stories.

A key to happiness is to give up our belief that circumstances have something to do with our happiness, so we can *see* that our inner happiness has everything to do with how we view circumstances.

Judgments

Judging others is just forgetting about separate realities, and deluding ourselves into *thinking* our reality is the right one. For everything we judge, someone else has been able to *see* the same event with compassion and understanding. Judgment is similar to the pot calling the kettle black, or "looking for the mote in the eye of another, when the beam in our own eye distorts our view." When we observe others through our judgment filters we are defining our own state of mind while believing we are defining theirs. Judgment is an indicator of our own lostness rather than of the lostness of the person we are judging. The person we are judging may be lost in thought-produced insecurity, taking some form of negativity, but if we ourselves were not lost, we would *see* the innocence and realize that person just doesn't know any better. We would feel compassion and understanding, instead of judgment, and might then be inspired to do something to make that person feel more secure, or else get out of the way without judgment.

Those who judge usually experience negative feelings within themselves, and blame them on whatever or whomever they are judging.

A key to happiness is to give up our judgments so we can *see* with compassion and understanding and experience peace of mind.

Expectations

Beauty can be right in front of us, and can be better than what we think we want, but we miss it when we are focused on expectations. Therefore, whenever we narrow our vision to expecting certain (even wonderful) outcomes, we greatly increase the probability of disappointment.

A key to happiness is to give up our expectations so we can *see* and enjoy what is.

Assumptions

Assuming we know what someone else is thinking or experiencing is really a joke. We have missed a deep understanding of separate realities when we give credi-

167

bility to our assumptions. When we base our own thoughts and feelings on our assumptions about what someone else thinks and feels, we react to our assumptions and blame others for what we think they think. It is humorous when we *see* it.

A loving mother relinquished custody of her children so they would not be torn apart in a court battle. She then assumed that people would judge her harshly and lived in fear of what others would think. Some did judge her harshly, but a majority of the people with whom she shared her experience reacted with compassion and statements of empathy: "That is the ultimate in unselfishness" "What a sacrifice" "That must have been a painful decision" "You must really miss them." She finally realized that either she could tailor her life around the judgmental people and live with fear and feelings of inadequacy, or she could live her life from her natural state of mind and appreciate those who saw her circumstances with understanding. When she gave up her assumptions that everyone would be the same, she discovered the many different ways she and others could be.

A key to happiness is to give up our assumptions and live life freshly, moment to moment, from our natural state of mind.

Beliefs and Realities

Alfred Adler once said, "Ideas have no meaning except the meaning we give them." We often attach such importance to the meaning we assign to our thoughts and ideas that they become beliefs we live and die for.

A firm belief in the flatness of the world does not make it so. Neither does believing water is clear because we can't see the microorganisms mean they are not there.

A key to happiness is remembering that beliefs and realities are creations of our thoughts. When we forget this, our creations will seem very real to us. But when we recognize them for what they are—just our way of seeing things for the moment—we won't be bound by them.

So much is missed when our focus is narrowed by the barriers we create in our thought system.

Barriers
When I remove my barriers
the beauty of
  what is
  of life
  of you
  of me
is overwhelming.

When I stop frustrating myself
  with expectations
    from life
    from you
    from myself

I am
  filled
  content
  at peace
    with my good fortune.

When we dismiss these and other barriers, such as *shoulds* and rules, we allow ourselves to be guided by inspiration from our natural state of mind.

SIGNPOSTS TO HAPPINESS

Signposts on our treasure map help us get past the barriers of our thought system to the experiential reality of our inner happiness and serenity.

Gratitude

Joe: "I can't see anything to be grateful for in this messed-up world."

Wise old Zeke: "I'll bet you would be a millionaire if I gave you $100 for everything you could think of to be grateful for."

You will see what you look for.

Gratitude is a natural feeling when negative thoughts have been dismissed. In higher levels of consciousness we *see* the beauty of life that is all around us and are filled with gratitude. When filled with gratitude we *see* clearly how silly it is to be upset by some of the little things we take seriously in a lower state of mind.

When first learning about the principles I felt disappointed in myself every time I got lost in thought. As my understanding increased, I stopped taking this seriously and had compassion for myself. Now I even feel a sense of gratitude when I get lost because I know I will come out of it with greater understanding. Every time I get off track and experience my judgments or any other form of negativity, the experience confirms that being lost in thought is not a pleasant place to be, and my understanding deepens. You can imagine how much more pleasant lostness is when feeling gratitude rather than when taking it seriously and judging yourself. The lostness keeps getting shorter and shorter.

It is impossible to feel gratitude and negativity at the same time. My *understanding* of that truth lets me know that it makes sense to focus on what I am grateful for, rather than on what I have been thinking about to make myself unhappy. Sometimes when I catch myself in negative thought I start singing "Oh What a Beautiful Mornin'." Unhappiness is dismissed, and happiness comes flooding in.

A key to happiness is allowing yourself to *see* the miracles all around you with gratitude.

Compassion

Feeling compassion is another natural occurrence when we *see* what thought is. With perspective we *see* the innocence in others and know that they do the very best they can from their present level of understanding.

A key to happiness is allowing ourselves to experience the compassion from our natural state of mind that makes it easy to forgive ourselves as well as others.

What We See or Feel or Give Is What We Get

When we are in a low mood and feeling judgmental or angry, we are stuck with those feelings. When we are in a high mood and *see* the innocence of all behavior, we have feelings of love, compassion, and understanding;

171

we have peace of mind. When we give love, that is what we get. We don't have to get it from someone else, because love is inherent in the feelings we have when we give love.

A key to happiness is understanding that we reap what we sow.

Love and Understanding

The greatest key of all is love. When we feel loving, we see beauty and positivity in everything. All that is needed to solve any problem we can imagine is love.

Love and *understanding* are the same thing. Love without *understanding* is conditional (not love at all).

With understanding we *see* thought for what it is. With understanding it is impossible to judge. With understanding we have compassion. With understanding we have peace of mind and contentment. With understanding we have beautiful feelings, which will guide us to respond appropriately in every situation. With *understanding* we have love.

Remember that *understanding* is not about *shoulds*. Suppose you don't feel loving? So what? What you feel is what you feel, based on your present level of understanding. *"Shoulding"* on yourself about that just makes it worse. *Understanding* usually changes what you feel, but if you try to change it through *shoulds* you block *understanding*.

A key to happiness is listening to your inner wisdom until *understanding* sneaks past your thought system.

The Battle between Love and Ego

Love is the ultimate reality; ego is the ultimate illusion.
Ego is the need to prove self-importance, which is based
on the illusionary belief in insecurity. It is the source of
jealousy, self-righteousness, possessiveness, judgment,
expectation, revenge, depression, stress, and disease.

What power this illusion of ego can create.

Love has a greater power: love heals every problem. Through the perspective of love, problems disappear. Love fills us with feelings that guide us to solutions
that make the problem seem insignificant.

Joe chided Zeke, "All this talk of love sounds like
religion and the flower children from the sixties to me. It
really turns me off."

Wise old Zeke replied, "Could it be that the reason
you don't have much love in your life is because it turns
you off?"

A key to happiness is recognizing the difference
between love and ego so that ego can be dismissed and
love can be enjoyed.

Enjoying What Is While It Is

Have you ever looked back at a time in your life and
thought, "I was really happy then. Too bad I didn't
realize it so I could have enjoyed it more"?

Have you known others who did not appreciate
what they had until they lost it?

Have you known others who thought their circumstances were a tragedy, but later saw them as the best
thing to have happened to them?

When we *understand* the principles, the beauty of life is profound. What used to seem insignificant or taken for granted is seen with appreciation and gratitude. We are often so filled with beauty, contentment, and the wonder of life that we have no choice except to get quiet and enjoy it.

I got a glimpse of life today
    beyond my thoughts
        and was filled
            with wonder
            with beauty
            with peace
    and gratitude.

A key to happiness is to enjoy what is.

Happiness and Serenity

What could be more important than happiness and serenity? When happiness is what we want, it makes no sense to entertain thoughts that lead in any other direction.

Can you imagine the wonderful revolution that will take place when we all start laughing at the many silly thoughts that create so much misery?

This key to happiness is so simple. *Dismiss negative thoughts and you have happiness and serenity.*

AS A MAN THINKETH, SO IS HE.

For information on ordering books by Jane Nelsen,
see the last page of this book.

BOOKS AND TAPES BY JANE NELSEN

To: Sunrise Books, Tapes & Videos   Telephone: 1-800-456-7770
        P.O. Box B   (Orders only please)
        Provo, UT 84603

BOOKS	Price	Quantity	Amount
UNDERSTANDING by Jane Nelsen	$9.95	_____	_____
POSITIVE DISCIPLINE by Jane Nelsen	$10.00	_____	_____
RAISING SELF-RELIANT CHILDREN IN A SELF-INDULGENT WORLD by H. Stephen Glenn and Jane Nelsen	$9.95	_____	_____
I'M ON YOUR SIDE by Nelsen & Lott	$9.95	_____	_____
TIME OUT: ABUSES AND EFFECTIVE USES by Jane Nelsen & H. Stephen Glenn	$6.95	_____	_____

MANUALS/STUDY GUIDES	Price	Quantity	Amount
TEACHING PARENTING MANUAL by Jane Nelsen and Lynn Lott	$29.95	_____	_____
EMPOWERING TEENAGERS AND YOURSELF IN THE PROCESS STUDY GUIDE (included with Empowering Teenagers tape set) by Lott and Nelsen	$10.00	_____	_____
POSITIVE DISCIPLINE STUDY GUIDE (included with Positive Discipline Video) by Jane Nelsen	$6.00	_____	_____

CASSETTE TAPES	Price	Quantity	Amount
POSITIVE DISCIPLINE by Jane Nelsen	$10.00	_____	_____
EMPOWERING TEENAGERS AND YOURSELF IN THE PROCESS by Lynn Lott and Jane Nelsen (seven-tape set)	$49.95	_____	_____
UNDERSTANDING: The Book On Tape by Jane Nelsen (Read by Gina Dupre)	$19.95	_____	_____

VIDEOS	Price	Quantity	Amount
POSITIVE DISCIPLINE by Jane Nelsen	$49.95	_____	_____

SUBTOTAL _____

Sales tax: UT = 6.25%; CA = 7.25% _____
Shipping & Handling: $2.50 first item; 50¢ each item thereafter _____
TOTAL _____
(Prices subject to change without notice.)

METHOD OF PAYMENT (check one):
_____ Check or Money Order made payable to SUNRISE, INC.
_____ Mastercard _____ Visa
Card #_____ _____ _____ _____   Expiration _____/_____

Ship to_____
Address_____
City/State/Zip_____
Daytime Phone_____